WILLIAM SHARP

ENGRAVER.

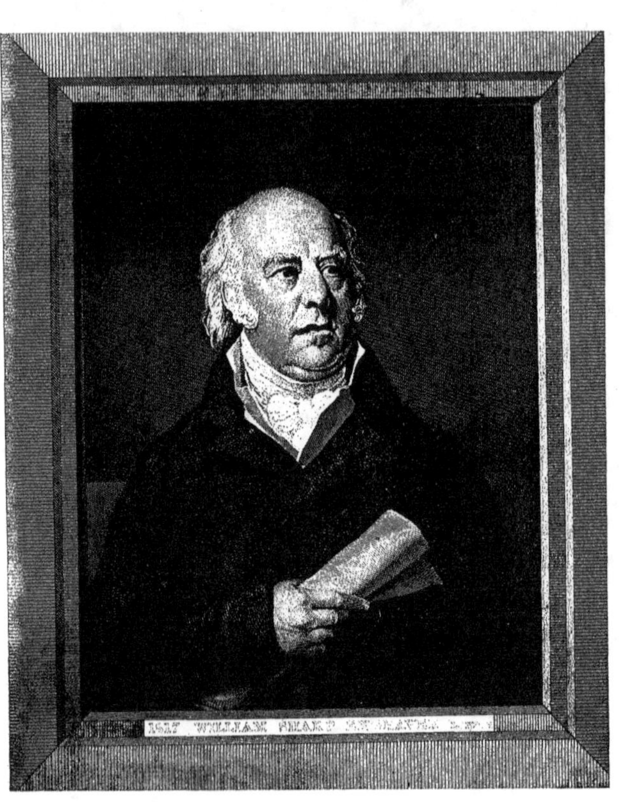
WILLIAM

WILLIAM SHARP

ENGRAVER

WITH A

DESCRIPTIVE CATALOGUE

OF

HIS WORKS

BY

W. S. BAKER

PHILADELPHIA
GEBBIE & BARRIE PUBLISHERS
1875

TO

JOHN S. PHILLIPS, Esq.,

FOR WHOSE VARIED INFORMATION, MENTAL VIGOR, AND PERSONAL CHARACTER, I ENTERTAIN THE HIGHEST RESPECT,

This Work

IS MOST SINCERELY INSCRIBED,

BY HIS FRIEND,

W. S. BAKER.

May, 1875.

WILLIAM SHARP

ENGRAVER

IF a school of art may be said to secure a foundation and attain a positive existence, when its disciples, striking out a new path, follow it successfully step by step, and gradually develop all its intrinsic merits, then we may safely say, that the English school of engraving sprang into being when the mezzotinto method was introduced into that country.

This new manner of engraving, practiced but little on the Continent, seems to have been at once appropriated by the English engravers; for to use the words of John Evelyn, who published the secret in the year 1662, having received it from Prince Rupert, to whom it was imparted by the inventor, Ludwig von Siegen, "it set so many artists to work that they soon arrived to that perfection it is since come, emulating the tenderest miniatures."

In their hands, beginning with John Smith and George White (two good English names), the resources of this style were so fully brought out that it came to be called the English method, and even in our own day, the engravers in mezzotinto of England hold the same relative position in the art, as those who practiced it in the seventeenth and eighteenth centuries. What this development has been is sufficiently proved by a mere allusion to the works of such men as McArdell, Houston, Earlom, Pether, Green and Murphy, of the last century; and Say, Hodges, Ward, Turner and Cousins, of the present.

Previous to this time (1662), and even up to the beginning of the last century, the line engravers of England, limited almost entirely to portraiture, produced but little (with the exception of those admirable artists, Hollar and Faithorne) of sufficient merit or consequence to stand the test of the ripened judgment of the connoisseur of the present day. But the eighteenth century witnessed the perfection of a branch, to the English practitioners, of which we are indebted for some of the finest productions of the art. Francis Vivares, John Browne, William Woollett and others, have left us works which have never been surpassed, and place the landscape engravers of the English school at the head of all others. Not but that the Continental schools have produced individual examples of great excellence, but such are only isolated cases, not sufficient, of themselves, to overcome the aggregate talent of the English.

But the salient point of this period, and one revealing the fullest strength of the English school of line engraving, is found in the works of its historical engravers, the principal of whom, it is our purpose to particularly notice, whose works, for simple dignity, force and directness of purpose, have rarely, if ever, been equalled. We allude to William Sharp, the greatest historical engraver that England has yet produced.

William Sharp was born in London, on the 29th day of January, 1749. Evincing at an early age, an inclination to drawing, his father, a gun-maker, of some repute, determined to qualify him for that branch of engraving, which he deemed the most important, the ornamenting of fire-arms.

He was accordingly apprenticed to a Mr. Longmate, who practiced this species of engraving, technically termed *bright* engraving, from the attention being drawn to the work; and not to impressions taken from it, by filling the incisions with ink.

At the expiration of his engagement, and with this limited preparation for prosecuting the art beyond mere business purposes,—having in the meantime married a French woman,—he commenced for himself.

The early efforts of a man of talent are always interesting, but in the case of the subject of our notice, they become of more than usual importance, inasmuch as there is no evidence of his having at any time received any positive or actual instruction in the higher walks of his profession. He may be classed among those who have worked themselves into distinction by their native powers of observation, perseverance and industry, the progress towards excellence being regular and certain. The varied powers exhibited in his works show a constant desire for improvement, and great freedom from the constraint of any regular manner or school. He was the founder of his own style, the intelligent pupil of his own labor and experience.

His first attempts at engraving for the purpose of taking impressions therefrom, were two business cards, designed for attracting attention to his regular vocation. The one a vignette of an angel seated among clouds, wearing a wreath of laurel, and holding a circular tablet, on which is inscribed "Sharp, Engraver, No. 9 Bartholomew Lane, Royal Exchange, London;" the other a small oval, consisting of two figures, one standing, the other seated on a cloud, a wreathed circle is between them, bearing the same inscription as the former, and on a ribbon which they hold "History, Ornamental Writing, Seals, &c." Both of these cards are well engraved.

His next essay is of much greater interest, both as an evidence of his desire to become something more than an engraver of dog collars, and door and card plates, and as being the first real step towards superior art. It is a quarto plate, published 1775, and from his own drawing, of an old lion "Hector," well known at the time as an inmate of the tower of London, the prints from which being exposed for sale in his shop window, attracted considerable notice, and sold moderately well. The drawing offers no evidence of future ability, but the engraving is well done, and shows considerable command of the burin.

Encouraged by the sale of the "Hector" print, he was induced to relinquish his original calling, and seeking more eligible quarters, moved to the neighborhood of Vauxhall, where he began to engrave small plates for book publishers, thus commencing his career as an artist, a career in which, in the words of a contemporary writer, "he performed some of those grand and laborious works, which will long remain an honor to himself, his art and his country." At this period of his life he is described as a well-formed, well-looking man, inclining to corpulence, laboring zealously in his profession, fond of out door exercise, and indulging in daily ablutions in the Thames, being a strong and expert swimmer. For neighbor and occasional associate he had John Browne, the distinguished landscape engraver.

The first plate to bring him into notice, as an historical engraver, was that of "Alfred the Great, dividing his loaf with the Pilgrim," after Benjamin West, executed for, and published by Alderman Boydell, in 1782. It has considerable merit, shows good drawing—it is said he was instructed in this branch by West—and is well engraved, yet scarcely prepares one for the admirable production of two years later, the "Lucretia" after Dominichino, also published by Boydell.

The "Lucretia" is a splendid example of the art, executed in the firmest, freest, and broadest manner, every stroke clear and distinct, not a line too much, not a line too little. Carefully and laboriously engraved, yet free from all appearance of mechanism, and so consecutive in all its parts, that it seems almost to be the production of a single sitting. It was a fit prelude to his great work of the following year, 1785, "The Doctors of the Church," after Guido Reni.

The picture formerly in the Houghton gallery, now in the Imperial gallery at St. Petersburg, painted for Paul V., represents the four Latin Doctors of the Church, St. Jerome, St. Ambrose, St. Augustine and St. Gregory, arguing and consulting their great books for the authorities on the subject of the favorite doctrine of the Catholic Church, the "Immaculate Conception," which was confirmed by that Pope in a bull issued in 1617; with them are presented St. John Damascene and St. Ildefonso, who were especial defenders of the doctrine.

This picture, painted in Guido's early and more powerful manner, was eminently suited to the innate vigor of the engraver, and his translation of it is a work of art in its truest sense. Every part of it is managed with the most consummate skill, and in the finest keeping; the drapery well and nobly arranged, the deep thought and character of each head admirably rendered, the anatomy most carefully developed, and the drawing perfect; a profound sense of meditation pervades the whole, well fitting the character of the scene. Sharp considered it his best work.

It forms the cap-piece of his reputation; and well might Raphael Morghen say to its engraver, after exhibiting the choice, reserved proofs of his own numerous fine productions, well might he say, as he drew from his folio an impression of the justly celebrated plate, "And now, Mr. Sharp, I will show you a print which is equal to anything I ever did in my life!" It is something when one artist can appreciate the work of another; but we know that the Italian *never* produced its equal.

The exquisite little oval print of this time, 1786, "The Children in the Wood," after a drawing by Benwell, of which he engraved the figures, the landscape being engraved by Byrne and Medland, deserves more than a passing notice, not alone for its merits, but for exhibiting a power of adaptation as well to his subject as to the treatment of his co-workers. The figures of the two children asleep in a close wood are most carefully and delicately engraved, in a manner suited to their youth and innocence, as it is to the fine sentiment and execution of the landscape, and did we not know otherwise, the same hand would seem to have produced the whole plate.

While thus constantly employed and establishing his reputation as an engraver, he became dissatisfied with the remuneration which he received from the print dealers, and becoming possessed of some property, by the decease of a brother, he began to publish his own works. Soon afterwards about the year 1787, that date appearing on his print of "Zenobia," he moved to a larger house in Charles street, near the Middlesex hospital.

This print, a profile after a picture, by Michael Angelo, in the possession of Sir Joshua Reynolds at the time of the engraving, is one of the best efforts of the engraver. It shows a wonderful command of the burin, and is fully up to the most exacting demands of the art. Every portion of it, the flesh, the head attire, the decorations are executed in the most appropriate manner and with the utmost taste and ability, while the calm dignity of the illustrious queen is most happily rendered. Nothing is slighted, nothing forgotten, and we are told that it was a great favorite of the engraver himself.

It was about this time—the removal to Charles street—that the even tenor of his life was disturbed, and the serenity of his mind became unsettled, with those singular hallucinations regarding the *prophet* Richard Brothers, and the folly, if not crime, of Joanna Southcott. The delusion of this lunatic Brothers consisted in imagining that he was divinely appointed to gather the Jews together and to lead them on their predestined march to recover Jerusalem. Sharp engraved his portrait, with rays of light descending upon his head and with the title of 'Prince of the Hebrews,' the sincerity of his belief in the rhapsodies of the *prophet* is made manifest by the sentence inscribed beneath, 'Fully believing this to be the man whom God has appointed I engrave his likeness, William Sharp.' The would-be *Prophet* however died in a madhouse leaving his mission unaccomplished.

In his belief in the pretensions of Joanna Southcott, he was not alone, for it is said that at one period the number of her converts in London, and its vicinity, amounted to upwards of a hundred thousand. She was a woman of humble parentage, born in 1750, and when about forty years of age, being carried away by the fervor of a heated imagination, gave herself out as the woman mentioned in the 12th Chapter of the Book of Revelation. In this her assumed capacity, although in the highest degree illiterate, she scribbled much mystic and unintelligible nonsense in the way of vision and prophecy, and for a while carried on a lucrative trade in the sale of seals, which were, under certain conditions, to secure the salvation of the purchasers. Her followers became very enthusiastic, but about the close of the year 1814, the time of her death, she herself began to have misgivings, during some comparatively lucid intervals, in which she declared that 'if she was deceived, she was convinced she had at all events been the sport of some spirit either good or evil.'

Sharp engraved her portrait from his own drawing, and is said to have believed in her till the day of his death. She is represented sitting, with an open book before her, and wears a large bonnet, somewhat different in shape and size from the female headgear of the present day. There is a complacent, self-satisfied look in her broad and fleshy countenance, while the eye has an unmistakable expression of low cunning.

The last survivor of the followers of Joanna Southcott, a certain Mrs. Peacock, on whom the mantle of the prophetess was supposed to have fallen, died quite recently at the advanced age of one hundred and three years.

The simplicity of his nature which brought him under the influence of these delusions, served him however to much better advantage on a certain and rather important occasion, and relieved him from an unpleasant, and at that time, dangerous predicament. Dabbling a little (it could be no more) in the politics of Thomas Paine and Horne Tooke—both of whose portraits he engraved—he was brought before the members of the privy council as one suspected of entertaining revolutionary principles. During his examination, being vexed at what to him seemed irrelevant questions, he handed to Pitt and Dundas the prospectus of a work which Tooke had in contemplation, requesting them to have the goodness to put their names to it as subscribers, and then to give it to the other members of the council to add theirs. A hearty laugh at the singularity of the proposal ensued, and he was soon after liberated.

From the great number of portraits that are being daily, nay hourly produced, a large proportion of which it must be admitted are very common place, the majority of observers, not reflecting that it is given but to few to attain excellence, fall into the error of supposing that portrait painting is an inferior branch of the art. Now the exact reverse is the truth, for when properly understood and prosecuted it is one of the highest. The portrait painter, to be successful, must be a close observer of nature, possess a keen insight into mind and character, and a faculty to perceive and, when perceived, to express all those little indications and traits of temperament and habit which, when transferred to the canvass, impress us with a full sense of individuality.

All the great painters of history were fine portrait painters, and their portraits are prized not wholly as admirable examples of painting, but also as exponents of life and character, each furnishing as it were by masterly interpretations, an epitome of humanity, an easily read page of history.

Thus something more is needed than dexterous management of material; mind must seek mind, so that the "ruling passion" may be discovered and expressed. If such are the elements of portrait painting, and if such are the requisites of a portrait painter, must not the translator possess in a degree, corresponding faculties, in order to enable him to convey in his language, that which the painter expresses in his, the original.

Portrait engraving is the most usually practiced form of the art, but portrait engraving, when prosecuted according to these rules, and with this intelligence is one of the highest branches of the art, and in this William Sharp stands unrivalled in the English, and the equal of the best portrait engravers of any school.

His earliest dated portrait (1777), is a small circular plate of Alderman George Faulkner, very roughly executed; but his very earliest, judging from the work itself, is an unfinished one of Dr. Samuel Johnson, still smaller. It is engraved in the very rudest manner, without any attempt at middle tint or regularity of line, yet preserves some indications of resemblance to the well known features of the famous lexicographer.

Of the large portraits engraved by Sharp, two are always especially referred to and quoted as fine examples, both of the art and the artist. The 'John Hunter,' of the year 1788, and 'Matthew Boulton,' of 1801.

The former painted by Sir Joshua Reynolds, represents the eminent surgeon and distinguished anatomist, seated at a table in an easy and natural position, in the act of inditing a manuscript, the head slightly raised, with the eyes turned upwards as in thought. With the exception of the hand holding the pen, the broken lines of which seem scarcely satisfactory, every part of this plate is executed in the very best manner, the drawing perfect, every line in its proper place to give character and expression, the face and hair being most delicately engraved. The striking characteristic of the work being the faithful rendering of 'the pale cast of thought,' which makes the countenance one not easily forgotten. The late Charles Sumner, a great lover and excellent judge of prints, terms this 'the foremost portrait in English art, and the coëqual companion of the great portraits of the past.'

The latter 'Matthew Boulton,' after a painting by Sir William Beachey, represents that celebrated engineer, also seated, a three-quarter length, with a medallion portrait in one hand, and an examining glass in the other. This is engraved with a broader line, and in a more vigorous manner than the former, eminently adapted to the character and personality of the successful manufacturer and active partner of James Watt, the distinguished improver of the steam engine. As in the John Hunter, every part of the plate is carefully engraved and skilfully managed, conveying the idea of a strong, healthy organization, coupled with the markings of firmness and self reliance, traits of character which he must have possessed. Well do these works deserve the esteem in which they are held, each different, yet each remarkable in its way.

Sharp had some eccentric notions on the subject of physiognomy. He advanced the singular doctrine that every man's countenance had depicted on it the appearance of some bird or beast, to the character of which his natural disposition bore a resemblance. Thus in those whose dispositions were generous and courageous, he fancied he could discover the likeness of a lion ; in those who were fierce, he saw that of tigers or eagles, whilst the timid and hesitating betrayed the characteristics of the milder and more gentle type of animals. He made no scruple in the personal appropriation of these resemblances, and his comparisons were sometimes highly amusing.

Besides the two large portraits already mentioned, there are others of the same size, quite, if not equal in merit. Of these that of 'The Right Reverend Samuel Seabury, D. D.' Bishop of Connecticut, after Thomas Spence Duché, published in 1786, is of interest as being the portrait of the first Protestant Episcopal Bishop of the United States, painted by the son of the Reverend Jacob Duché, so well remembered for his course during our revolutionary struggle. The Bishop, a half-length in robes, is standing with his left hand extended, as if speaking, while his right rests easily on a closed Bible placed on some rocks, the back ground being made up of a landscape. It is executed in Sharp's best manner, and is a splendid specimen of portrait engraving.

We may cite also that of 'The Right Hon. Robert Dundas, President of the Court of Session,' after Raeburn, published 1790, with the one of a few years later of 'The Hon. John Hyde, one of the Puisne Judges of the Supreme Court at Calcutta, in Bengal,' after R. Home, in wig and gown, in which the fair complexion of the judge is most admirably rendered, and the engraving in every respect of the finest character.

Of his later period, and fully equal to anything he has done, is the 'Sir Everard Home,' after Sir William Beechy, of the year 1810, nearly a full length sitting, a masterly work; and 'Sir Francis Burdett, Bart,' after James Northcote (1811), a half length, the head and figure full of character, and the flesh tints most admirably given. It is engraved in the same manner and is as fine as the highly esteemed one of 'Matthew Boulton.'

Of his smaller portraits that of 'Kemble,' after Martin Arthur Shee, (1803), may be mentioned; and of his smallest 'The Hon. Thomas Erskine,' and 'George, Prince of Wales,' both after miniatures by Richard Cosway. The latter is an exquisite production, engraved in the most tender and delicate manner, and in a fine early impression is a perfect gem.

We close our reference to his portraits with one of exceeding interest apart from its merits as an engraving, which are of the highest order. It is from the portrait of Charles I., painted by Vandyk for the purposes of Bernini the sculptor, in which he is represented in three positions, profile, three-quarter and full face. No one can look at this print without being touched with the sorrowful cast of the countenance, and being impressed with the innocence of the unfortunate king. It is a sad, sad page of English history, brought vividly, almost painfully before us.

But it is as an historical engraver, that Sharp's great ability and varied powers are made manifest, to thoroughly comprehend which, it is only necessary to examine for a few moments his two prints, the 'Lear,' after Benjamin West, and 'The Doctors of the Church,' already referred to. No two works are more unlike, the one a representation of the absolute repose of deep thought, the other an expression of the violent action of overpowering feeling, 'the tempest of the mind.' The effect of the one rendered by the boldest exercise of line and sudden transitions of light and dark, the other indicating by careful and deliberate markings in all its parts, the absorption of reflection and absence of excitement. We have designated one as forming the cap piece of his reputation, but the 'Lear,' for vigor and originality of execution has never been surpassed, and when West insisted that it should not be engraved in the chalk manner, but in line, and by Sharp, he not only asserted the dignity of his own art, but showed a proper appreciation of the professional excellence of the engraver.

Leslie in speaking of Boydell's well known enterprise, the 'The Shakespeare Gallery,' for which the picture was painted, says 'It did also much for engraving; and, among other admirable productions, we owe to it Sharp's transcendent work from West's 'Lear,' a work showing that the power of a first-rate engraver, even of other men's designs, does not lie within the scope of mere talent; but that it is *genius*, and of a higher order than that displayed by many a painter, who looks upon engravers as artists much below him.'

For pictorial qualities as well as an example of Sharp's wonderful executive ability, the print of 'Diogenes in search of an honest man,' after Salvator Rosa, is justly celebrated. The rugged countenance of the old cynic is marked with all the certainty of time itself, while the flowing beard and ample drapery are engraved in the most admirable manner.

His 'St. Cecilia,' after Dominichino, though stiff and formal in its character, and displaying perhaps a little too much of the handicraft of the engraver, is nevertheless a noble production, but as a work of the painter, it fails in giving that expression of rapt inspiration which of right belongs to the countenance of one who hears 'the music which is divine.'

Quite different again in subject, but of exceeding merit as an engraving, and unsurpassed in its truth of translation, is the 'Head of Christ,' after a remarkable painting by Guido. The picture, or rather sketch in oil—in possession of Benjamin West at the time of the engraving—is said to have been produced with unprecedented and almost incredible rapidity. It represents the Saviour, crowned with thorns, the hair thick and clammy with sweat and blood, drops of which have fallen upon his breast; the expression which is most wonderfully translated in the engraving, is that of resignation under agony. 'Behold! and see if there be any sorrow like unto his sorrow.' The varied manner of line, the deep rich tone so ably imparted, and the entire handling, evincing the fullest sympathy with the subject, make this an extraordinary production, in which the engraver has carried his art to its highest development, and completest purpose.

Other well known works are the 'Infant

Christ' after Annibale Carracci; the large plate of 'The Holy Family,' after Sir Joshua Reynolds; 'The Witch of Endor,' after Benjamin West; and the smaller but very beautiful one of 'The Virgin and Infant Saviour,' after Carlo Dolci.

His largest plates are 'The Sortie made by the Garrison of Gibraltar,' after John Trumbull, most of the heads in which are elaborate portraits, and 'The Siege and Relief of Gibraltar,' after J. S. Copley; the former has been pronounced one of the finest historical engravings of modern events that has ever been executed.

But to specify Sharp's best works, is simply to enumerate all, and a selection is either a matter of taste or a choice of subject. Few engravers have been so equal, yet so varied, few translators so true, yet so original.

His professional fame was widely spread even in his own time, and in 1814 he was elected a member of the Imperial Academy at Vienna, and of the Royal Academy of Bavaria. Sir Joshua Reynolds offered to recommend him as an associate engraver of the Royal Academy, London, but he rejected the offer, warmly espousing the opinions of Sir Robert Strange, Woollett, Hall, and other eminent engravers who considered their art slighted by their not being allowed to become Royal Academicians.

His last important plate was the 'Mary Magdalene,' after Guido, the finished print being dated 1822, the seventy-fourth year of his age, a beautiful work which shows but little evidence of failing powers, the defective execution of the chin, and the drapery on the right shoulder being the most apparent; a large fine plate of the same year, 1822, 'The Women at the Sepulchre,' from a picture by Annibale Carracci, was left unfinished.

He died at Chiswick on the 25th day of July, 1824, and lies buried in the Church yard at that place with Hogarth and De Loutherbourg, for the latter of whom, he at one time entertained much mystic reverence, for possessing as a follower of Mesmer, a half-physical, half-miraculous power of curing diseases and imparting the thoughts and sympathies of distant friends. Sharp left no descendants, his wife having died at an early period of their married life without issue.

What a singular contradiction is presented in the life and works of England's celebrated engraver, and what a forcible illustration of the alternate strength and weakness of our nature do they reveal to us. His works, are the exponents of prolonged energy and mental dignity, every line a thought, and every thought clothed in the noblest language of the art.

The life, how different! The engraver of "John Hunter" and "The Doctors of the Church," is found to be a superstitious believer in the wild prophecies of a lunatic, a blind devotee to the cunning devices of an ignorant woman. We rise from contemplating his works, feeling that we have been in communication with an earnest, honest man; our ideas have been enlarged, and our reverence for truth has been increased. We peruse the record of his life, and are saddened and humiliated with its story of weakness and credulity.

> "What thin partitions sense from thought divide!"

But the life of a man of genius, the life of William Sharp, must be sought for in his works. Throughout all may be discovered a simple earnestness and determined integrity of purpose, a resolve to do that which was allotted him, and to do it well, which carries instant conviction of moral strength and purity of life; that he may have been practiced on, but could not practice on others, and that an unsuspecting faith in the honesty of his own nature, precluded him from suspecting that of others.

Long after the names of Richard Brothers and Joanna Southcott, shall have been forgotten, and the folly of their adherents remembered only with wonder and regret, will the productions of the engraver be sought for and prized, and his character as truly exhibited in them, be perceived and appreciated.

That which man feels, that only he expresses; the truth or error which is within becomes apparent in the handiwork.

A

DESCRIPTIVE CATALOGUE

OF

THE WORKS

OF

WILLIAM SHARP

ENGRAVER.

PREFACE.

The following catalogue is claimed to be a full record of the life work of "William Sharp, Engraver," whose career exemplifies in the most striking manner, the fact that talent is simply labor intelligently directed.

It was compiled with but two exceptions, the portrait of "Sir William Hamilton," and the "Entrance Ticket for a Vauxhall Regatta," from the singularly complete collection of that artist's productions in the possession of John S. Phillips, Esq., of Philadelphia, from which source most of the different states of the plates were obtained, some from one or two other collections, and a few from good authorities being included.

While not as complete in this direction, as could be wished, it may be considered reliable as far as it goes, and is thus offered to those interested in the subject, and as being really the first descriptive catalogue of the works of one whose prints must always form an important feature in every well selected general collection.

The measurements, which are in English inches, refer to the engraved portions of the plate, the margins not being included, except in one instance, which is noted.

W. S. B.

SCRIPTURAL SUBJECTS.

1. **THE ANGEL DESTROYING THE ASSYRIAN CAMP.** 2 Kings, xix., 35. J. P. DE LOUTHERBOURG, R. A. PINXT.

Height, 12 inches; width, 9 8-10th inches.

1. Before all letters, unfinished.
2. Before the title, the engraver's name only, in traced letters.
3. Title in open letters, with the scriptural reference. *London, Published Oct'r 5, 1792, by Thos. Macklin, Poets' Gallery, Fleet Street.*

2. **JUDITH ATIREING.** Judith, Ch. 10, Ve. 1, 2, 3. J. OPIE, R. A. PINXT.

Height, 12 inches; width, 9 8-10th inches.

1. Before all letters.
2. Title in open letters, with the scriptural reference. *London, Publish'd July 21st, 1794, by Thos. Macklin, Poets' Gallery, Fleet Street.*

3. **THE WITCH OF ENDOR.** Vide the 1st Book of Samuel, 28th Chapter & 14th verse. PAINTED BY B. WEST, HISTORICAL PAINTER TO HIS MAJESTY.

Height, 16 8-10th inches; width, 23 1-10th inches.

1. Before all letters, unfinished.
2. Before the title, the artists' names, and *London, Publish'd June 20, 1788, by Thos. Macklin, No. 39 Fleet Street,* in traced letters.
3. Title in finished letters, with the scriptural quotation and reference, and the dedication to Daniel Daulby, Esq.
4. Title in finished letters. *London, Publish'd by J. & J. Boydell, No. 90 Cheapside, & at the Shakespeare Gallery, Pall Mall.*

4. **INFANT CHRIST.** ANN. CARACCI, PINXT.

Height, 9 inches; width, 7 inches.

1. Before all letters.
2. Before the title, the engraver's name only in traced letters.
3. Title in open letters. *London, Published by William Miller, MDCCCXI.*
4. Title in finished letters, without the address.

5. **THE VIRGIN AND INFANT SAVIOUR.** CARLO DOLCI, PINXT. Up. oval in rectangle.

Height, 9 6-10th inches; width, 7 7-10th inches.

1. Before all letters, unfinished.

2. With the scriptural quotation in cursive letters, and with the artists' names. *From the original Picture in the possession of Rich'd Sullivan, Esq. Publish'd by Wm. Sharp, London, Dec. 15, 1797.*
3. With the date in the address, *1798.*

6. **THE HOLY FAMILY.** SIR JOSHUA REYNOLDS, PINXT.

Height, 22 inches; width, 17 9-10th inches.

1. The etching, with engraver's name in traced letters.
2. Before all letters, unfinished, engraver's name only in traced letters.
3. Before the title. *London, Publish'd Aug. 12, 1792, by Thos. Macklin, Poets' Gallery, Fleet Street.*
4. Title in open letters.
5. Title in finished letters. *From an original Picture in the collection of Sir Peter Burrell.*

7. **THE HOLY FAMILY.** SIR JOSHUA REYNOLDS, PINXT. The smaller plate.

Height, 12 inches; width, 9 8-10th inches.

1. Before all letters, unfinished.
2. Before all letters.

3. Title in open letters. *Frontispiece to the New Testament*, in open letters. *Published Feb'y 12th, 1793, by Thos. Macklin, Poets' Gallery, Fleet Street, London.*
4. Title in finished letters. The address, *Frontispiece*, &c., omitted.

8. **THE AGONY OF CHRIST.** St. Luke, Ch. xxii., V. 42. RICHARD COSWAY, PINXT.

Height, 12 inches; width, 9 8-10th inches.

1. Before all letters.
2. The title "Christ's Passion," in open letters and with the scriptural reference. *Published March 1, 1791, by Tho. Macklin, Fleet Street.*
3. The title in finished letters.

9. **HEAD OF CHRIST**, crowned with thorns. GUIDO, PINX. Up. oval with border, in rectangle.

Height, 9 6-10th inches; width, 7 6-10th inches.

1. The etching, before the rectangle, the border indicated with a single line.
2. With the inscription in cursive letters; in the border at the top in Roman letters, "Behold, and see if there be any sorrow like unto his sorrow." *From the original Picture in the possession of B. West, Esqr. Published by W. Sharp, London, Dec. 25, 1797.*
3. With the date in the address, *March 18, 1798.*

10. THE MARYS AT THE SEPULCHRE. Mark Ch. xvi., V. 5. R. SMIRK, PINXT.

Height, 12 inches; width, 9 8-10th inches.

1. Before all letters unfinished.
2. Before all letters.
3. Before the title, engraver's name only in traced letters.
4. Title in open letters, with the scriptural reference. *London, Published July 16, 1791, by Thos. Macklin, Fleet Street.*

11. THE WOMEN AT THE SEPULCHRE.

Height, 20 inches; width, 23 3-10th inches.

1. Before the title, unfinished. *Publish'd by Will'm Sharp, London, Feb'y 10, 1822,* in dotted letters.
2. Title in open letters, with the address in dotted letters. *From the Picture by Annibale Carracci, in the collection of the Earl of Carlisle.* To the extreme right, beneath the print the words *Holy Thursday,* in dotted letters. *Engraved by William Sharp, and printed in the state in which it was left at his decease.*
3. Title "The three Maries and the dead Christ," in open letters, with the dedication to the Earl of Carlisle. *Engraved by Wm. Sharpe. Finished by F. Bacon. London,*

published by Herring & Remington, 137 Regent Street, London, Jan'y 1, 1850, & Goupil & Vibert, Paris; Artaria & Fontaine, Mannheim.

12. **MARY MAGDALENE.** "Mary hath chosen that good part, which shall not be taken from her," Luke 10., V. 43. GUIDO, PINXT.

Height, 9 5-10th inches; width, 7 7-10th inches,

1. Before the border at the bottom of the print and the scriptural quotation. Artists' names in traced letters. *Publish'd by William Sharp, London, May 16, 1820.*
2. Before the border and quotation, the artists' names in dotted letters, date in address, *May 16, 1821. From the original picture in the possession of Sir Simon H. Clark, Bart,* in dotted letters.
3. The border indicated by a single line, artists' names, address and reference to ownership of picture in dotted letters.
4. With the border filled in, and the scriptural quotation and reference introduced. The title, in the inscription in the margin in open letters. Date in the address, *16 May, 1822.*
5. Title in inscription in finished letters.

HISTORICAL SUBJECTS.

13. **THE DOCTORS OF THE CHURCH,** Consulting upon the Immaculateness of the Virgin. St. Luke, Chap. I, verse 49. GUIDO RENI, PINXIT, GEORGE FARRINGTON, DELINT.

Height, 22 9-10th inches ; width, 15 4-10th inches.

1. Before the arms and all letters.
2. Before the motto in the arms and before all letters.
3. Before the title, artists' names only in traced letters.
4. Before the title, the artists' names, and *Publish'd Sept. 1, 1785, by John Boydell, Engraver in Cheapside, London,* in traced letters.
5. Title in open letters.
6. Title in finished letters, with the scriptural reference. *In the Gallery at Houghton.*

14. **A CHERUBIM.** From "The Doctors of the Church." Up. oval, unfinished.

Height, 7 5-10th inches; width, 6 4-10th inches.

15. ST. CECILIA. Three-quarter length, crowned with roses, and attended by two angels, in her right hand the palm of martyrdom. PAINTED BY DOMINICHINO.

Height, 19 inches; width, 14 9-10th inches.

1. The etching.
2. The title, "Cecilia," in open traced letters, and before the border, artists' names in traced letters. *Published May 1790, by W. Sharp, No. 8 Charles Street, Midd'x Hosp'l.*
3. With the border, the day of the month, *10*, introduced in the address.
4. The title, "St. Cecilia," in open letters. *From a picture in the possession of Rob't Udny, Esqr.* Date in the address, May *20*, 1790, with the addition of *Wm. Skelton, Haymarket, & Chr. Towes, 119 Cheapside.*
5. The title, in finished letters.

16. ST. CECILIA. The same picture engraved in 8vo.

Height, 6 inches; width, 4 5-10th inches.

1. The etching, artist's names only, in dotted letters.
2. Title "Subscribers' ticket to the second series of the select work of engravings, under the direction of William Buchanan, Esq.," in open letters. *London, 1 Feb'y, 1814, Pub'd by Ar. Stone, 87 Pall Mall.*

17. BOADICEA HARANGUING THE BRITONS. OPIE, R. A. PINXT

Height, 11 4-10th inches; width, 8 2-10th inches.

1. The etching.
2. Before all letters.
3. Title in open letters. *Published by R. Bowyer, Historic Gallery, Pall Mall, Nov'r, 1795.*

18. BOADICEA THE BRITISH QUEEN, ANIMATING THE BRITONS TO DEFEND THEIR COUNTRY AGAINST THE ROMANS. T. STOTHARD, R. A. DELT. Arched top with ornamented spandrils.

Height, 10 8-10th inches; width, 13 4-10th inches.

1. Before the title. *Engraved & pub'd by W. Sharp, from a drawing by T. Stothard, R. A., Dec. 20, 1811,* in traced letters.
2. Title in open letters, dated in address, altered to *January 28, 1812.*
3. Title in finished letters.

19. ALFRED THE GREAT, DIVIDING HIS LOAF WITH THE PILGRIM. PAINTED BY B. WEST, HISTORICAL PAINTER TO HIS MAJESTY.

Height, 17 inches; width, 23 4-10th inches.

1. Before the arms and all letters.
2. Title in open letters with arms. *Published as the act directs, November 9th, 1782, by John Boydell, Engraver in Cheapside, London.*

3. Title in finished letters, with the dedication "To the Master Wardens," &c.

20. THE INTERVIEW OF CHARLES THE FIRST WITH HIS CHILDREN, during his misfortunes, in the Presence of Oliver Cromwell. SAM'L WOODFORDE, R. A. PINXIT.

Height, 19 inches; width, 23 inches.

1. The etching. *Published by Will'm Sharp, London, May 1818,* in traced letters.
2. Before the title, with the artist's names, the address in dotted letters, the date altered to *May 16, 1820.*
3. Title in open letters.
4. Title in finished letters, with the dedication to His Most Gracious Majesty, George the Fourth. *London, Published Jan'y 29th, 1821, by Will'm Sharp, Member of the Imperial & Royal Academy at Vienna, & of the Royal Academy of Bavaria.*

21. KING CHARLES THE 2nd, LANDING ON THE BEACH AT DOVER. PAINTED BY B. WEST, HISTORICAL PAINTER TO HIS MAJESTY.

Height, 16 3-10th inches; width, 23 3-10th inches.

1. The etching.
2. Before all letters, with the four white Flags.
3. Before all letters, the Flags finished.

4. The title "Restoration" in open letters, with the name of William Sharp as engraver. *Etch'd by Wm. Woollett, Historical Engraver to his Majesty. Published as the act directs, April 5, 1789, by B. West, E. Woollett, & J. Hall, London.*
5. Title in finished letters. *From the original Picture in the possession of The Right Honourable the Earl Grosvenor.*

22. Q. MARY'S ESCAPE FROM LOCHLEVEN CASTLE. PAINTED BY R. SMIRKE, R. A.

Height, 11 4-10th inches; width, 8 3-10th inches.

1. Before all letters.
2. Title in open letters. *Published by R. Bowyer, Historic Gallery, Pall Mall, Jan'y, 1795.*

23. THE SORTIE MADE BY THE GARRISON OF GIBRALTAR, in the morning of the 27th of November, 1781. PAINTED BY JOHN TRUMBULL, ESQ.

Height, 19 8-10th inches; width, 30 2-10th inches.

1. The etching.
2. Before the title, the artist's names only in traced letters.
3. Title in open traced letters.
4. Title in open letters. *Published Jan'y 1, 1799, by J. Trumbull, W. Sharp, & A. C. dePoggi, No. 91 New Bond Street.*

5. Title in German text. *London, Published Jan'y 1, 1799, by J. Trumbull, Esq'r, No. 72 Welbeck Street, A. C. dePoggi, No 91 New Bond Street, and by W. Sharp, No. 8 Charles Street, Middlesex Hospital.*

24. **THE SIEGE AND RELIEF OF GIBRALTAR,** (in two compartments), J. S. COPLEY, ESQ., R. A. & F. A. A. PINXT.

Height, 22 8-10th inches; width, 32 2-10th inches.

1. Before all letters, unfinished.
2. Title in open letters, before the dedication.
3. Title in finished letters, with the dedication "To the King's most excellent Majesty, &c." *London, Published March 27th, 1810, by J. S. Copley, George Street, Hanover Square.*

25. **VIGNETTE,** for Bowyer's edition of Hume's England. Three Nereides at the foot of a high rock, hung with medallion portraits of naval heroes. R. SMIRKE, DEL.

Height, 10 5-10th inches; width, 7 5-10th inches.

2d April, 1800, by R. Bowyer, London, in traced letters.

26. **LOUIS VII., KING OF FRANCE, BEFORE BECKETT'S TOMB.** MARIA COSWAY, PINXT.

Height, 11 5-10th inches; width, 8 3-10th inches.

1. Before all letters.
2. Title in open letters. *London, Published by R. Bowyer, Historic Gallery, Pall Mall, March, 1800.*

27. DIOGENES IN SEARCH OF AN HONEST MAN. SALVATOR ROSA, PINXT.

Height, 16 5-10th inches; width, 13 4-10th inches.

1. Before all letters.
2. Before the title, the engraver's name only in traced letters.
3. Before the title and before the painter's name. The engraver's name, and *Publish'd 1st April, 1792, by Wm. Sharp, London,* in traced letters.
4. Title in open letters.
5. Title in finished letters. "From an original Picture in the possession of Edw'd Knight, Esq'r." *Published April 18, 1792, by Wm. Sharp, London. Sold by John Murray, Fleet Street, B. B. Evans, Poultry, Molteno & Co., Pall Mall, W. Skelton, Hay Market.*

28. LUCRETIA. Three-quarter length, in the act of stabbing herself. DOMENICHINO, PINXT. Oblong oval in a rectangle.

Height, 12 7-10th inches; width, 17 inches.

1. Before all letters, the flesh parts unfinished.
2. Before all letters.

3. Before the title, with the artist's names. *John Boydell, excudit, London, 1784. Published June 1st, 1784, by John Boydell, Engraver in Cheapside, London,* in traced letters.
4. Title in open letters.
5. Title in finished letters, with the inscription reciting the story. *In the collection of The Right Hon. Welbore Ellis.*

29. ZENOBIA. Profile head and bust. MICHEL ANGELO BUONAROTA, PINXT. Without inclosing lines or background. Size of plate,

Height, 10 7-10th inches; width, 8 2-10th inches.

1. Before the title, artist's names, and *Published March 1, 1787, by Will'm Sharp, London,* in traced letters.
2. Title in Greek letters. *Engraved from an original Picture in the possession of Sr. Jos'a Reynolds,* in heavy cursive letters. *London, Publish'd, 1st Jan'y, 1788, by W. Sharp, No. 8 Charles Street, Middlesex Hospital, B. B. Evans, corner of old Jewry, Cheapside, & W. Skelton, No. 23 Haymarket.*
3. Title in Roman letters. *Published Jan'y 1, 1799, by William Sharp, London.*

30. HERO AND LEANDER.

Height, 9 9-10th inches; width, 7 9-10th inches.

1. Before all letters, unfinished.

31. **KING LEAR.** Act I., Scene I., PAINTED BY R. SMIRKE.

Height, 10 7-10th inches; width, 6 5-10th inches.

1. Before all letters.
2. Title in open letters.
3. Title in finished letters. *Publish'd Octo. 6, 1792, by J. & J. Boydell, Shakspeare Gallery, Pall Mall, & No. 90 Cheapside.*

32. **KING LEAR.** Head and bust. Up. oval in rectangle.

Height, 6 4-10th inches; width, 5 5-10th inches.

Title in finished letters. "Engraved by Wm. Sharp from a Picture of Sr. Joshua Reynolds." *Publish'd May 1st, 1783, by John Boydell, Engraver, in Cheapside, London.*

33. **SHAKSPEARE. KING LEAR.** Act III., Scene IV. PAINTED BY B. WEST, ESQ'R, R. A., & PRESID'T OF THE ROYAL ACADEMY.

Height, 17 5-10th inches; width, 23 4-10th inches.

1. The etching, with the title "Shakspeare," in open letters, artist's names, and *Publish'd June 4, 1792, by J. & J. Boydell, at the Shakspeare Gallery, Pall Mall, & No. 90 Cheapside,* in traced letters.

2. Finished impression without the title or painter's name. *Etch'd by Sharp*, in traced letters. The latter part of the address only with difficulty perceived.
3. Title in open letters, with the artist's names and address, the date altered to *March 25, 1793*.
4. Title in finished letters, with the quotation, *off, off, you lendings, &c.*

34. ROMEO AND JULIET. Act III., Scene VII. "ENGRAV'D BY W. SHARP, FROM A PICTURE OF B. WEST, ESQ'R."

Height, 5 1-10th inches; width, 6 5-10th inches.

Publish'd June 24, 1783, by John Boydell, Engraver, in Cheapside, London.

35. MERRY WIVES OF WINDSOR. Dr. Caius discovering Simple in his closet. "ENGRAVED BY WILLIAM SHARP, FROM A DRAWING BY ROBERT SMIRKE. Up oval.

Height, 6 inches; width, 4 5-10th inches.

London, Publish'd Feb'y 1, 1784, by Charles Taylor, No. 8 Dyer's Buildings, Holborn.

36. MERRY WIVES OF WINDSOR. Act V., Scene V. "Falstaff between Mrs. Page and Mrs. Ford." PAINTED BY R. SMIRKE.

Height, 9 2-10th inches; width, 6 5-10th inches.

1. Before all letters.
2. Title in open letters. *Publish'd Dec. 24, 1793, by J. & J. Boydell, Shakspeare Gallery, Pall Mall & Cheapside.*

37. RICHARD 3d. Act V., Scene III. PAINTED BY J. OPIE, R. A.

Height, 9 9-10th inches; width, 8 2-10th inches.

Title in open letters. *Publish'd Aug. 1, 1794, by Mr. Woodmason, Leadenhall Street, London.*

LARGE PORTRAITS.

38. **CHARLES THE FIRST, KING OF GREAT BRITAIN, &c. &c. &c.** In three positions, profile, three-quarter and full face. ANTONIUS VANDYCK, EQUES PINXIT.

Height, 8 5-10th inches; width, 9 7-10th inches.

1. The etching.
2. The title in open cursive letters, with the words *in aqua forti fecit,* after "Vienna," in the engraver's honorary title. *London, Pub'd 1 Nov., 1813, for the Select work of Engravings, intended to illustrate the Portraits and Ideal Characters of the Great Masters of the various schools of Painting, under the direction of Wm. Buchanan, Esq'r. By Mr. Dixon, Jun'r, at the Historick Gallery, 87 Pall Mall.*
3. The title in finished Roman letters, with the word *sculpsit* instead of "in aqua forti fecit," and directly beneath the print in dotted letters, the date *Aug't 12, 1817.* The date of the address (in which there is a slight difference of wording), is 1st Feb'y, 1815.

39. THOMAS HOWARD, EARL OF ARUNDEL. Half length sitting, landscape to the right. VAN-DYCK, PINXIT.

Height, 10 2-10th inches; width, 8 inches.

1. The etching in a forward state, the title in open letters. After "Vienna," in the engraver's honorary title, the words *in aqua fortis fecit. London, 1 October, 1814, Pub'd at the New Gallery, 60 Pall Mall, for the Select work of celebrated Portraits and Illustrious characters. By Wm. Buchanan, Esq'r.*
2. Title in open letters, not quite finished, with the address, and *in aqua fortis fecit.*
3. Title in open letters, with the word *sculpt* instead of "in aqua fortis fecit." "From the original picture in the possession of the Marquis of Stafford." *London, 1 July, 1823, Pub'd by John Dixon, at his Printing office, No. 29 Tottenham Street, for the Select work of engravings under the direction of Wm. Buchanan, Esq'r.*
4. Title in finished letters.

40. SIR FRANCIS BURDETT, BART. Half length, right hand resting on an upright volume labelled "Magna Charta." JAMES NORTHCOTE, R. A. PINXT.

Height, 16 7-10th inches; width, 13 inches.

1. Before the title, with the artist's names. "Engraved from a Picture painted during his imprisonment in the Tower," in open letters, *and Published by Wm. Sharp, 27 London Street, Fitzroy Square, Feb'y 14, 1811,* in traced letters.
2. Title in open letters, with the reference and address.

41. **SIR WILLIAM CURTIS, BART,** Alderman & Representative of the City of London. Full length, sitting in an arm chair, right hand resting on a table; to the right a view of the Sea, a ship introduced. THOMAS LAWRENCE, ESQ'R, R. A. PINXT.

Height, 22 1-10th inches; width, 13 6-10th inches.

1. The etching.
2. Before all letters, and the arms.
3. Before the title and arms, but with the artist's names.
4. Title in open letters, with the arms. *Publish'd by W. S. Blake, Change Alley, London, March 1, 1814.*

42. **SIR WALTER FARQUHAR, BART.** Full length, sitting to the right in an arm chair, hands clasped. PAINTED BY H. RAEBURN. Private plate.

Height, 16 7-10th inches; width, 13 6-10th inches.

1. Before all letters.
2. Title in finished letters, with the artist's names.

43. THE RIGHT HON'BLE ROBERT DUNDAS. Lord President of the Court of Session. Nat., 29 July, 1713; ob., 13 Dec., 1787. Three-quarter length, sitting in judicial robes, left hand on a table. PAINTED BY H. RAEBURN.

Height, 16 7-10th inches; width, 13 5-10th inches.

1. The etching in a forward state.
2. Before the title and border, with the artist's names. *London, Publish'd March 1, 1790, by Wm. Sharp, No. 8 Charles Street, Middlesex Hospital,* in traced letters.
3. Title in open letters, the month in the address, *May,* with the addition of *Wm. Skelton, Hay Market, & John Murray, Book Seller, Fleet Street, London,*

44. THE HON'BLE JOHN HYDE, one of the Puisne Judges of the Supreme Court at Calcutta, in Bengal. Three-quarter length, sitting in judicial costume, holding in his right hand a pen, the left resting on a table. R. HOME, PINXIT.

Height, 17 2-10th inches; width, 13 7-10th inches.

1. Before all letters and the arms.
2. Title in open letters, with the arms. *Published Jan'y 1, 1800, by R. Home, of Calcutta, & Wm. Sharp, of London.*
3. Title in open letters, with the engraver's name as member of the Imperial & Royal Academy of Vienna. *London, 25 March, 1814, Published by Mr. Arthur Stone, at the Historic Gallery, 87 Pall Mall.*

45. ROBERT HOPPER WILLIAMSON ESQ'R, Chancellor of the County Palatine of Durham, and Recorder of New Castle upon Tyne. Half-length sitting.

Height, 13 inches; width, 10 7-10th inches.

1. The etching, before the border or arms.
2. Before all letters, border or arms.
3. Title in open letters, with the arms and the inscription.

46. THE RIGHT REVEREND SAMUEL SEABURY, D. D., BISHOP OF CONNECTICUT. Three-quarter length standing in robes, right hand resting on a closed Bible on a heap of rocks. Landscape background. THOS. S. DUCHE, PINXT.

Height, 17 inches; width, 13 1-10th inches.

Title in open letters, with the dedication "To Benjamin West, Esq'r, R. A., Historical Painter to His Majesty." *Publish'd April 20th, 1786, by T. S. Duche, at the Asylum, Lambeth & J. Phillips, George Yard, Lombard St.*

47. CHARLES BURNEY, D. D., F. R. S., & S. A., Rector of Cliffe & of St. Pauls, Deptford, Kent; Prebendary of Lincoln, & Chaplain in ordinary to his Majesty. Half length, in robes, full face. Private plate.

Height, 13 inches; width, 7 7-10th inches.

1. Before all letters, unfinished.

2. Before all letters.
3. Before the title, the engraver's name in the border in traced letters. *Publish'd, London, Dec. 1, 1821*, in dotted letters.
4. The title in finished letters. *Prebendary, &c.*, in open letters. The engraver's name below the border, in regular engraved letters.

48. MATTHEW RAINE, D. D., F. R. S., & S. A. Half length, in gown and wig; full face. J. HOPPNER, ESQ'R, R. A., PINXT.

Height, 12 6-10th inches; width, 10 8-10th inches.

1. The etching.
2. Title in open letters. Below the title "One of the Senior Fellows of Trinity College, Cambridge; Head Master of Charterhouse School; Preacher of Gray's Inn, & Rector of Little Hallingbury." *Published Dec. 1, by Wm. Sharp, London, 1815*, in traced letters.

49. RICHARD HART DAVIS, ESQ'R, M. P., F. R. S. Half length, full face, wearing a coat with fur collar. SR. THOS. LAWRENCE, R. A., PINXT. Private plate.

Height, 12 6-10th inches; width, 10 7-10th inches.

1. Before all letters, unfinished.
2. Before the title and arms, engraver's name only in dotted letters.

3. Before the title and arms, artist's names in dotted letters.
4. Title in open letters, with the arms, artist's names in dotted letters.

50. FILMER HONYWOOD, ESQ'R. M. P. Nearly full length sitting, holding with both hands a paper headed "Kent Petition, 1780." Through an opening to the left, a landscape.

Height, 13 3-10th inches; width, 11 inches.

1. The etching.
2. Before all letters.
3. Title in finished letters. *London, Engraved & Published by Will'm Sharp, April, 1804.*

51. EDWARD JENNER, M. D., F. R. S., &c., &c., &c. Three-quarter length, sitting in an arm chair. W. HOBDAY, PINXIT.

Height, 16 5-10th inches; width, 13 3-10th inches.

1. Before all letters, unfinished.
2. Before the title, the painter's name, and *W. Skelton, aqua forti fecit* in traced letters.
3. Title in finished letters, with the dedication to the King by the painter. In the middle of the margin next the print, *Begun by the late Will'm Sharp,* to the right, *Will'm Skelton sculpsit. London, Published Jan'y 2, 1826, by R. Ackermann, 101 Strand.*

52. **SIR EVERARD HOME.** Nearly full length, sitting, right hand resting upon a table on which are papers and writing materials, a manuscript in his left hand. SIR WM. BEECHY, PINXT. R. A.

Height, 16 6-10th inches; width, 13 5-10th inches.

1. Before all letters.
2. Before the title, artist's names in traced letters.
3. Before the title, artist's names in traced letters. *Published Octo. 25, 1810, by Will'm Sharp, London,* also in traced letters.

53. **JOHN HUNTER.** Head and bust, head supported by left hand. REYNOLD'S, PINX.

Height, 5 6-10th inches; width, 4 6-10th inches.

London, Published, Jan'y 1, 1788, by W. Sharp.

54. **JOHN HUNTER.** Three-quarter length, sitting in an arm chair, the right hand holds a pen, the left supports his head, the elbow resting on a table. SIR JOSHUA REYNOLD'S PINXT.

Height, 16 6-10th inches; width, 13 5-10th inches.

*1. Before all letters.
2. Before the title, the artist's names, and the address in traced letters.
3. Before the title, artist's names, and *London, Publish'd 1st Jan'y, 1788, by Wm. Sharp, Charles Street, Midd'x Hospital,* in engraved letters.

* There are said to be ten different states of this plate.

4. Title in open letters.
5. Title in finished letters, with the addition to address of *B. B. Evans, corner of the old Jewry, Cheapside, & W. Skelton, No. 23 Hay Market.*

55. **RICARDUS PORSON.** Head and bust; head in profile. J. HOPPNER, R. A., PINXT.

Height, 12 5-10th inches; width, 10 8-10th inches.

1. The etching.
2. Before all letters.
3. Before the title, the artist's names in traced letters. *Published Nov. 4, 1810, by Will'm Sharp, London,* in dotted letters.
4. Title in open letters.

56. **THE HON'BLE LT. COL. CHARLES CATHCART.** Half length, in uniform. G. ROMNEY, PINXT.

Height, 9 inches; width, 7 3-10th inches.

1. Before the title. In the middle of the margin, *Gulielmus Sharp, Sculpsit, Londini, Januarius 1, 1791.*
2. Title in open letters traced with the point, with artist's names and date.

57. **THADDEUS KOSCIUSZKO.** Full length, reclining on a sofa. "ENGRAVED BY WILLIAM SHARP, FROM A MODEL IN WAX DONE FROM THE LIFE BY C. ANDRAS."

Height, 12 1-10th inches; width, 15 inches.

1. Before all letters unfinished.
2. Before all letters.
3. Title in open letters.
4. Title in finished letters. *Published as the act directs, 1st Feb'y, 1800, for C. Andras, at Mr. Bowyer's, the History Gallery, Pall Mall, Mr. Alderman Boydell, Cheapside, & Mess. Colnaghi, Sale & Co., Cockspur Street.*

58. KEMBLE. Half length, sitting, left elbow on a table, the hand on his breast directly in front. M. A. SHEE, R. A., PINXT.

Height, 10 2-10th inches; width, 8 6-10th inches.

1. Before letters or border.
2. Before letters, with the border.
3. Title in open letters. *London, Published by W. Sharp, April 7, 1803.*
4. Title in finished letters.

59. WILLIAM SHARP, ENGRAVER. Half length, full face, holding a roll of manuscript in his right hand. PAINTED BY G. F. JOSEPH, A. R. A.

Height, 12 inches; width, 10 inches.

1. Before letters, and before the border.
2. Before letters, the tablet in the lower border, blank.
3. Before the title, the tablet blank. In the margin, *London, Published May 12, 1817, by John Smith, Princes Street, Cavendish Square.*

4. Title in tablet in open letters, to the left "1817," and to the right "London," also in open letters.
5. Title in shaded letters, with the tablet filled in. *London, Published Sept. 1, 1819, by Hurst, Robinson & Co., (late Boydell's,) 90 Cheapside.*

60. **JOANNA SOUTHCOTT.** Half length sitting, an open book before her, a large bonnet on her head. DRAWN AND ENGRAVED FROM LIFE BY WM. SHARP.

Height, 11 9-10th inches; width, 9 8-10th inches.

1. Before all letters.
2. Before the title. In the tablet in the lower border, to the left "Isaiah, Ch. LXV. & LXVI.," to the right "Jan'y, 1812," in open letters. *Published by Jane Townley, London.*
3. Title, date, &c., in open letters.

61. **THOMAS PAINE.** Half length, three-quarter face. Upon a table to the left, pamphlets entitled "Rights of man," & "Common Sense." ROMNEY, PINXT.

Height, 10 5-10th inches; width, 8 5-10th inches.

Title in open letters, in the lower border. *London, Published by W. Sharp, No 8 Charles Street, Midd'x Hosp't, April 20, 1793.*

62. **THOMAS PAINE.** The smaller plate, same picture.

Height, 3 8-10th inches; width, 3 1-10th inches.

Title in finished letters. *London, Pub. Feb'y 1, 1794, by W. Sharp, No. 8 Charles Street, Midd'x Hosp't.*

63. **MR. BERESFORD.** Half length sitting. C. G. STEWART, PINXT. Up. oval in rectangle.

Height, 11 inches; width, 9 inches.

1. The etching.
2. Before all letters.
3. Before the title, with the artist's names. *London, Published by W. Sharp, March 25, 1796.*

64. **MATTHEW BOULTON, ESQ'R, F. R. S. & F. S. A.** Three-quarter length, sitting in an arm chair, in his left hand a medallion portrait, in the right an examining glass. SIR WM. BEACHEY, PINXT. Private plate.

Height, 16 6-10th inches; width, 13 3-10th inches.

1. Title in open letters, with the artists' names. *Published May 1, 1801, by Wm. Sharp, London.*
2. Title in finished letters, with the address.

65. **SAMUEL MOORE.** Half length standing at a table, holding in his right hand a paper entitled "Premiums offered in 1796, by the Society for the encouragement of arts, manufactures and commerce." B. WEST.

Height, 16 7-10th inches; width, 13 6-10th inches.

1. Before all letters.

66. **MAYOW WYNELL-MAYOW, ESQ.** Half length, three-quarter face. THOS. LAWRENCE, ESQ'R, R. A., PINXT.

Height, 10 5-10th inches; width, 8 8-10th inches.

1. Before all letters and arms.
2. Title in open letters, with the arms. Below the title "Died 14th January, 1807, aged 53." *London, Publish'd, April, by Wm. Sharp*, in traced letters.

67. **RICHARD REYNOLDS**, of the Society of Friends, late of Bristol. Half length, full face, sitting in a library, a Bible in his right hand. W. HOBDAY, PINXT.

Height, 13 3-10th inches; width, 10 7-10th inches.

Title in open letters, with the dedication and the inscription "Whose Life and Fortuue were devoted to the Glory of God by relieving the humble in Distress." In the border at the top, in open letters, "When the eye saw him it blessed him." *Published, Dec. 1, 1817, by Will'm Hobday, London.*

68. **THOMAS WALKER.** Full Bust. ROMNEY, PINXT.

Height, 10 4-10th inches; width, 8 5-10th inches.

1. Before the title and border, artist's names, and *Published Nov. 5, 1794, at No. 8 Charles Street, near Middlesex Hospital, London,* in traced letters.
2. Title in open letters in the border. *Published Nov. 5, 1794, by Will'm Sharp, Charles Street, near the Middlesex Hospital,* in traced letters.

69. **CHARLES LONG.** Half length, sitting in front of a table, upon which are writing materials. He wears a broad brimmed hat. Private plate.

Height, 10 inches; width, 8 inches.

1. Before all letters and border. This plate was afterwards altered, another head substituted without the hat. In the margin "E. L." in large cursive letters.

SMALLER PORTRAITS.

70. **GEORGE, PRINCE OF WALES.** Head and bust, head turned to right. Up. oval in an ornamented frame, surmounted with the plume of feathers, and surrounded by a radiance of glory. Beneath the oval in a scroll the motto "Ich Dien." R'DUS. COSWAY, PICTOR PRINCIPIS PINXT. GULIELMUS SHARP, SCULPSIT.

Height, 4 8-10th inches; width, 4 inches.

1. Before the frame, feathers and scroll, unfinished.
2. Before the frame, feathers and scroll, finished.
3. With the motto in the scroll in open letters, and with the frame and feathers. Artist's names in the frame. *Engraved & Publish'd by Wm. Sharp, No. 8 Charles Street, Middlesex Hospital, & sold by W. Skelton, Haymarket, Aug. 12, 1790.*

71. **GEORGE, PRINCE OF WALES,** 1791. From a bust by J. C. LOCHÉÉ.

Height, 7 1-10th inches; width, 4 4-10th inches.

1. Before the title. *Burney, del. Sharp, Sc.*
2. Title in open letters. *Published as the act directs.*

72. **THE DUKE OF CLARENCE.** Head and bust, three-quarter face to left. Up. oval in an ornamented frame.

Height, 4 7-10th inches; width, 4 inches.

1. Before all letters.

73. **GEORGE WASHINGTON,** Commander in Chief of ye armies of ye United States of America. Head and bust. In uniform. Up. oval in ornamented rectangle. The oval surmounted by a Liberty cap, beneath which is a rattle snake, in the border at the top, the legend "Don't Tread on Me."

Height, 6 3-10th inches; width, 4 3-10th inches.

1. Before all letters.
2. Title in finished letters. "Engraved by W. Sharp, from an original Picture." *London, Published according to act of Parliament, Feb'y 22, 1780.*

74. **SIR WALTER RALEIGH.** Head and bust. Circle in ornamented rectangle.

Height, 6 inches; width, 4 4-10th inches.

Title in open letters; engraver's name only. *Published by G. Kearsly, at No. 46 in Fleet Street.*

75. **OLIVER CROMWELL.** Head and bust, full face. In armor. Up. oval in ornamented rectangle.

Height, 6 9-10th inches; width, 4 5-10th inches.

"Engraved by W. Sharp, from an original Picture in the possession of R. Dalton, Esq'r." *London, Publish'd May 7, 1789, by T. Cadell, Strand,*

76. **HENRY WRIOTHESLEY, EARL OF SOUTHAMPTON.** Head and bust, full face, with a ruff around his neck. Up. oval, in ornamented rectangle. Beneath the oval a small ruined chapel, to the left, an up. vol. entitled "Shakespeare 1623."

Height, 5 8-10th inches; width, 3 6-10th inches.

1 Before all letters, face not quite finished.

2. Title in open letters. *London, Publish'd May 8, 1789, by J. Rivington & Partners.*

77. **SIR WILLIAM HAMILTON.** Proof before letters, 4 to. (Evans Cat. of Portraits, No. 16766.)

78. **THOMAS MARQUIS OF WHARTON.** Head and bust. Up. oval in ornamented rectangle.

Height, 6 inches; width, 4 5-10th inches.

79. **SIR JOHN WYNNE, BARONET.** Three-quarter length, standing.

Height, 5 6-10th inches; width, 4 5-10th inches.

80. **GEORGE MONK, DUKE OF ALBEMARLE.** Died 3d Jan'y, 1669–70, aged 67. Full bust in armor. Up. oval.

Height, 3 8-10th inches; width, 3 2-10th inches.

Eng'd for Hervey's Naval History, vol. II. page 317.

81. **GEORGE BYNG, LORD TORRINGTON.** Rear Admiral of Great Britain, Knight of the Bath, and First Lord of the Admiralty. Head and bust, flowing wig. Up. oval in ornamented rectangle, below the oval the representation of a naval battle.

Height, 5 7-10th inches; width, 3 6-10th inches.

Engrav'd for Hervey's Naval History, vol. V., Book 8., Ch. 1.

82. **ROBERT BLAKE, ADMIRAL.** Died 17th Aug. 1657, age 59. Full bust, three-quarter face, with a quotation from Glover, "Thy name, &c." Up. oval.

Height, 3 8-10th inches; width, 3 2-10th inches.

Engraved for Hervey's Naval History.

83. **ADMIRAL LORD HOWE.** Head and bust in a circle. J. S. COPLEY, R. A., PINXT.

Diameter 3 3-10th inches.

Before the title. *London, Published May 22, 1810, by J. S. Copley, George Street, Hanover.*

84. **CAPT. BARRINGTON.** Head and bust in a circle. J. S. COPLEY, R. A., PINX.

Diameter 3 3-10th inches.

Before the title. *London, Published May 22, 1810, by J. S. Copley, George Str't, Hanover Sq'e.*

85. **CAPT. THOS. FORREST.** Orancayo of the golden sword. Half length, sitting before a table, his right hand resting upon an open chart. To the left a view of the Sea, with Siamese vessels. J. K. SHERWIN, DEL.

Height, 8 8-10th inches; width, 7 3-10th inches

Published by the author as the act directs, Jan'y 30, 1779.

86. **THE HON'BLE THOS. ERSKINE.** Head and bust. R'DUS COSWAY R. A., PINXIT. GULIELMUS SHARP, SCULPSIT. Up. oval.

Height, 4 inches; width, 3 5-10th inches.

1. Title in open letters. Beneath the oval in traced letters, *London, Publish'd May 2, 1791, by W. Sharp, No. 8 Charles Street, Midd'x Hosp't.* At bottom of plate, *sold by W. Skelton, Haymarket, Moltano & Co., Pall Mall, & B. B. Evans, Poultry.*
2. Title in finished letters. Beneath the oval, *London, Engraved and Publish'd by Wm. Sharp, Octo. 10, 1801.* The address at bottom of plate, *W. Skelton, &c.,* omitted.

87. **DRYDEN.** Head and bust, three-quarter face. Up. oval, in ornamented rectangle. G. KNELLER, PINXT.

Height, 6 inches; width, 4 4-10th inches.

Pub. by G. Kearsly, No. 46 Fleet Street.

88. **JOHN MILTON** Head and bust, full face. Up. oval in ornamented rectangle, beneath the oval, Adam and Eve in the Garden.

Height, 4 5-10th inches; width, 3 4-10th inches.

"Engraved by Wm. Sharp, after an original miniature by Samuel Cooper, the ornaments by G. B. Cipriani & E. F. Burney."

89. **HEAD OF SHAKSPEARE.**

Height, 4 9-10th inches; width, 4 inches.

1. Before all letters or border.

90. **DR. SAMUEL JOHNSON.** Head and bust. Up. oval.

Height, 1 9-10th inches; width, 1 5-10th inches.

1. Before all letters, unfinished.

91. **SIR ISAAC NEWTON.** Head and bust, full face, flowing wig. Circle in a highly ornamented rectangle. G. KNELLER, PINXT.

Height, 6 inches; width, 4 4-10th inches.

Published by G. Kearsly, No. 46 Fleet Street.

92. **RICHARD CUMBERLAND.** Head and bust.

Height, 3 1-10th inches; width, 2 5-10th inches.

1. Before all letters.

93. **RICHARD BENTLEY.** Head and bust, in robes. Up. oval.

Height, 4 7-10th inches; width, 3 7-10th inches.

1. Before all letters.

94 **JOHN BUNYAN.** Three-quarter length, sitting in robes, left hand on an upright "Holy Bible."

Height, 7 6-10th inches; width, 6 3-10th inches.

1. Before all letters, and before the border.
2. The title "Portrait of John Bunyan," in open letters. Below the title "Author of the Pilgrims' Progress." *London, Pub. Aug. 1819, by Hurst, Robinson & Co., (late Boydell's,) 90 Cheapside.*

95. **GUILELMUS CUMING, M. D.** Col. Reg. Med. Edinb, et soc. Antiq. utriusque Sod. Head and bust. BEACH, PINX., 1783. Up. oval.

Height, 3 1-10th inches; width, 2 7-10th inches.

1. Before all letters.
2. Title in open letters, with the motto "Rien rechercher, Rien regretter; ne se plaindre de Personne." *Sharp, sc., 1785.*

96. **DANIEL ISAAC EATON.** Half length, sitting. ABBOT, PINXT.

Height, 3 9-10th inches; width, 3 1-10th inches.

1. Before all letters.
2. Title in finished letters, with the motto, "Frangas non Flectes," in open letters. *Pub'd May 14, 1794, at the Cock & Swine, No. 74 Newgate Street, London.*

97. **RICHARD BROTHERS, PRINCE OF THE HEBREWS.** Half length, three-quarter face, wearing a cravat with a large bow. Rays of light descending upon his head from the left.

Height, 6 7-10th inches; width, 5 5-10th inches.

The title in open letters in the lower border. In the margin the words "Fully believing this to be the man whom God has appointed; I engrave his likeness, William Sharp," *Published at No. 8 Charles Street, Midd'x Hospital, London, April 16, 1795, by W. Sharp.*

98. **JOHN JOHNSON.** Three-quarter length, sitting with clasped hands. HAUGHTON, PINXT. Private Plate.

Height, 7 1-10th inches; width, 5 7-10th inches.

Before the title, artist's names in dotted letters.

99. **DAVID GARRICK.** Head and bust.

Height, 3 8-10th inches; width, 3 inches.

Title in open letters. "Drawn by T. Uwins from a Picture by Gainsborough, in the Town Hall, at Stratford upon Avon." *London, March 1823, Published by W. Walker, 5 Gray's Inn Square.*

100. **JOHN HORNE TOOKE.** Head and bust. Up. oval.

Height, 2 5-10th inches; width, 2 inches.

1. Before all letters.

101. MR. CARTER. Head and bust. Up. oval.

Height, 2 6-10th inches; width, 2 2-10th inches.

1. Before all letters.

102. ALDERMAN GEORGE FAULKNER. Head and bust. Circle with a narrow border.

Diameter, 3 7-10th inches.

Title in open letters, in the border at the top. In the lower margin divided by the engraver's name, *Publish'd as the act directs, Octo. 22, 1777.*

103. JOSEPH PLANTA, ESQ'R. "ENGRAVED BY W. SHARP, FROM A MEDALLION BY PISTRUCCI."

Diameter, 2 9-10th inches.

1. Before the title. *Sharp, sculp.*
2. The title in light cursive letters. *Published, Dec. 1, 1817, by W. Clark, Bond St.*
3. The title in heavy cursive letters, without the address.

104. C. HEIDEGGER. A mask.

Height, 9 1-10th inches; width, 6 7-10th inches.

The title in heavy cursive letters.

105. HEIDEGGER. Profile after death. Up. oval.

Height, 6 8-10th inches; width, 6 inches.

The title in finished letters.

106. LUNARDI. Head and bust. Up. oval.

Height, 5 8-10th inches; width, 3 6-10th inches.

1. Before all letters.

107. PROFILE HEAD. After Fuseli.

Height, 6 5-10th inches; width, 4 2-10th inches.

1. Before all letters.

108. HEAD OF AN OLD WOMAN. After Rubens.

Height, 4 6-10th inches; width, 3 3-10th inches.

1. Before all letters, unfinished.

109. FEMALE HEAD AND BUST. Up. oval.

Height, 2 7-10th inches; width, 2 2-10th inches.

1. Before all letters.

110. A PERSIAN PRINCE. Profile head and bust. Up. oval.

Height, 3 3-10th inches; width, 2 7-10th inches.

Before the title. *Sharp, Sculpt*, in traced letters.

VARIOUS SUBJECTS.

111. CUPID AND HIS MOTHER. L. E. V. LEBRUN, PAINTER.

Height, 12 3-10th inches; width, 10 4-10th inches.

Title in finished German text letters. "*Sarp, Engraver.*" *London, Publish. de March 1, 1789, by Smith, No. 17 Strogmorton Street.*

112. VENUS AND EUROPA. Horace, book 3rd, Ode 27. WEST, PINXT.

Height, 5 2-10th inches; width, 6 6-10th inches.

1. The title "Jupiter and Europa," with the artist's names.
2. The title "Venus and Europa," with the reference to Horace. *Published June 24, 1783, by John Boydell, Engraver, in Cheapside, London.*

113. NIOBE. From the first Picture on that subject. PAINTED BY RICHARD WILSON, ESQ'R, R. A.

Height, 17 3-10th inches; width, 24 4-10th inches.

1. The etching.

2. The title in open letters, with the reference to the picture in traced letters. "The figures engraved by Will'm Sharp." "The Landscape by Sam'l Smith." *Published as the act directs by S. Smith, No. 58 Castle Street, east Oxford Street, May 31, 1792.*
3. The title in filled letters, with the reference to the picture in open letters, and with the dedication. The word *London* at the beginning of the address.
4. The title in filled letters, with the reference to the picture in open letters. *Published June 4, 1803, by J. & J. Boydell, No. 90 Cheapside, and at the Shakspeare Gallery, Pall Mall, London.*

114. CIRCE. Half length, standing with her cup. DOMENICHINO, PINXIT. JOS'H BOYDELL, DELINT. Up. oval.

Height, 10 2-10th inches; width, 8 5-10th inches.

1. Before all letters and before the inclosing lines.
2. The title in open letters. *John Boydell, excudit, 1780.*

115. HECTOR IN THE TOWER. "W. SHARP, SCULP. BARTHOLOMEW LANE."

Height, 5 3-10th inches; width, 7 1-10th inches.

Publish'd according to act of Parliament, Jan'y 9, 1775, by Wm. Sharp, No. 9 Bartholomew Lane, Royal Exchange, London.

116. **LANDSCAPE.** With a cottage on the right foreground.

Height, 6 inches; width, 8 2-10th inches.

1. Before all letters.

117. **LANDSCAPE.** Hellesley Hill, near Chester, with a balloon passing over. STOTHARD, DELT.

Height, 7 3-10th inches; width, 5 5-10th inches.

1. Before all letters.

118. **THE CHILDREN IN THE WOOD.** "DRAWN BY J. H. BENWELL." "THE FIGURES ENGRAVED BY W. SHARP." "THE LANDSCAPE BY W. BYRNE & T. MEDLAND." Oblong oval.

Height, 7 5-10th inches; width, 9 5-10th inches.

The title, artist's names, and *Published as the act directs, 20th May, 1786, by W. Byrne, No. 79 Titchfield Street, London,* in traced letters.

119. **JOSEPH ANDREWS.** See book 3, Cha. 12. "DRAWN by T. HEARNE." "THE FIGURES ENGRAVED BY W. SHARP." "THE LANDSCAPE BY W. BYRNE & B. T. POUNCY." Oblong oval in rectangle.

Height, 11 8-10th inches; width, 13 6-10th inches.

1. Before all letters, the landscape finished, the figures only etched.

2. The title "Joseph Andrews 2d, Ple.," in open traced letters. The artist's names, and *London, Feb'y, 1788, publish'd as the act directs, by W. Byrne, No. 79 Titchfield Street,* in traced letters.
3. Title in finished letters.

120. EVIL. A male head with wildly agitated hair, and terrible character of countenance. MICHEL ANGELO BUONAROTA, PINXT. No back ground.

Height, 11 3-10th inches; width, 8 2-10th inches.

1. Before all letters.
2. Before the title. Painter's name, in traced letters. *London, Published by Will'm Sharp, Sept. 2, 1816,* in traced letters.

121. THE TWO MANIACS. Sculptured by Cibber, over the entrance to Bethlem Hospital. STOTHARD, DELT.

Height, 5 3-10th inches; width, 8 3-10th inches.

With the lines "Bethlemii ad portas se tollit dupla columna, &c." *Pub. as the act directs, June 4, 1783.*

122. MONUMENT TO HARDINGE.

Height, 14 inches; width, 17 inches.

1. Before the border, unfinished.
2. With the border. "By Charles Manning, Sculptor." *London, Pub'd March 25, 1813, by Sarah Manning.*

123. **DECLARATION OF RIGHTS.** STOTHARD, DEL. "To the Society for Constitutional Information, this plate is inscribed," in open traced letters.

Height, 20 4-10th inches; width, 14 inches.

TWELVE PLATES FOR CAPT. COOK'S LAST VOYAGE. J WEBBER, DEL. They occur in etchings, proofs and finished letters.

124. **A Man of Oonalashka.**

Height, 9 1-10th inches; width, 6 9-10th inches.

125. **A Man of Kamtschatka.**

Height, 9 1-10th inches; width, 6-9-10th inches.

126. **A Woman of Kamtschatka.**

Height, 9 1-10th inches; width, 6 9-10th inches.

127. **A Man of Mangea.**

He ght, 9 1-10th inches; width, 6 9-10th inches.

128. **A Man of Nootka Sound.**

Height, 9 1-10th inches; width, 6 9-10th inches.

129. **A Woman of Nootka Sound.**

Height, 9 1-10th inches; width, 6 9-10th inches.

130. **The Inside of a Winter Habitation in Kamtschatka.**

Height, 8 9-10th inches; width, 15 2-10th inches.

131. The Inside of a House in Nootka Sound.

Height, 8 9-10th inches; width, 14 7-10th inches.

132. The Inside of a House in Oonalashka.

Height, 8 7-10th inches; width, 14 7-10th inches.

133. Poulaho, King of the Friendly Islands, drinking Kava.

Height, 9 2-10th inches; width, 15 3-10th inches.

134. A Night Dance by Men in Hapaee.

Height, 8 9-10th inches; width, 15 3-10th inches.

135. A Night Dance by Women in Hapaee.

Height, 8 9-10th inches; width, 15 1-10th inches.

136. TWO NUDE SAVAGES. Male and female.

Height, 7 4-10th inches; width, 5 3-10th inches.

1. Before all letters.

137. ATHENS. JAMES STUART, INV., WM. COLLINS, FEC.

Height, 15 5-10th inches; width, 16 inches.

138. BRITANNIA. RALPH WILLETT, INV., WM. COLLINS, FEC. Oblong oval.

Height, 15 5-10th inches; width, 24 inches.

139. MOSES STRIKING THE ROCK.

Height, 7 2-10th inches; width, 4 4-10th inches.

140. **NEHEMIAH,** CHAP. II., V. III. "Why should not my countenance be sad," &c. B., WEST, DELT.

Height, 6 8-10th inches; width, 5 1-10th inches.

London, Printed for J. Bell's British Library, 20th March, 1782.

141. **PAN AND SYRINX.**

Height, 7 5-10th inches; width, 5 7-10th inches.

1. Before all letters.

142. **CLEANDER BRIBING CLEON.** J. STUART, DELT.

Height, 7 2-10th inches; width, 4 9-10th inches.

143. **CHAUCER, REVES TALE.** The Miller of Trompington and Two Scholars. DRAWN BY MORTIMER.

Height, 8 1-10th inches; width, 6 inches.

London, Publish'd Feb'y 12, 1787, by J. R. Smith, No. 31 King Street, Covent Garden.

144. **TASSO, JERUSALEM DELIVERED,** Scene from. STOTHARD, DELT.

Height, 6 inches; width, 4 1-10th inches.

145. **THE EARL OF SOMERSET.** H. L. INVT.

Height, 7 7-10th inches; width, 6 inches.

146. THE WOUNDED SPORTSMAN. STOTHARD, DELT. Oblong oval.

Height, 6 inches; width, 7 5-10th inches.

1. Before the title, artist's names in traced letters. *Published Jan'y 1, 1788, by W. Lowndes,* in traced letters.
2. The title "Sylph," at the top in open letters.

147. THE MUSE OF PHILOSOPHY, dispelling the clouds of ignorance from the Garden of Science. STOTHARD, DELT.

Height, 7 6-10th inches; width, 6 inches.

Before the title, artist's names in traced letters.

148. MERCURY PUTTING ON HIS SANDAL WINGS. FRONTISPIECE TO HORNE TOOKE'S "DIVERSIONS OF PURLEY."

Height, 7 3-10th inches; width, 6 inches.

1. Before all letters.
2. Motto "Dum brevis esse laboro, obscurus fio," in open letters. *Published Jan. 1, 1798, by John Horne Tooke, Wimbledon, Surry.*

149. PORTICO OF A GREEK TEMPLE.

Height, 6 5-10th inches; width, 9 3-10th inches.

150. GREEK COINS AND ANTIQUES. Two plates.

151. GRECIAN FRIEZES. Three plates.

152. A MASK. From the antique.

Height, 4 inches; width, 3 inches.

1. Unfinished.
2. Before letters, engravers name only.

153. HEAD OF A BOY. From marble.

Before letters, engravers name only.

154. FEMALE HEAD. From marble.

1. Before all letters.

SMALL BOOK PLATES.

155. ANNUNCIATION TO THE SHEPHERDS. See Page 350, Vol. 1. B. WEST, DELT.

Height, 5 3-10th inches; width, 3 inches.

156. A SCRIPTURAL SUBJECT. See discourse, XIV., Vol. II. B. WEST, PINXT.

Height, 5 4-10th inches; width, 3 1-10th inches,

157. NATHAN SAID UNTO DAVID. Unfinished.

Height, 5 2-10th inches; width, 6 6-10th inches.

158. ORPHEUS AND EURYDICE.

Height, 5 5-10th inches; width, 4 inches.

1. The etching.
2. Before all letters.
3. With the engraver's name and the lines "En Iterum crudelia retro Fata vocant, conditque natantia lumina somnus."

159. AN ASSEMBLY OF THE HEATHEN DEITIES ON MOUNT OLYMPUS.

Height, 5 5-10th inches; width, 4 inches.

Pub. by Verner & Hood, 1802.

160. FRONTISPIECE TO POEMS. Dedicated to Her Majesty, by H. L. Oblong oval.

Height, 5 inches; width, 6 inches.

161. THE TAKING OF THE FOUDROYANT BY THE MONMOUTH, 1758.

Height, 3 3-10th inches; width, 5 8-10th inches.

Hervey's Naval History, vol. 5, Book 7, Ch. 4.

162. PLAN OF THE TOWN AND FORTIFICATIONS OF GIBRALTAR.

Height, 3 6-10th inches; width, 6 2-10th inches.

Hervey's Naval History. Frontispiece, Vol. III.

163. ILLUSTRATION OF A GRECIAN LEGEND. J. STUART, DELT.

Height, 5 8-10th inches; width, 3 2-10th inches.

164. MRS. SIDDONS, as Euphrasia in the Grecian Daughter. Act V., Scene III.

Height, 5 5-10th inches; width, 3 4-10th inches.

Pub. by W. Lowndes, April 10, 1783.

165. MISS BRUNTON, as Monimia in the Orphan. Act V., Scene II. STOTHARD, DELT. Ad. vivum.

Height, 5 2-10th inches; width, 3 4-10th inches.

Pub. by W. Lowndes, April 8th, 1786.

SEWARDS ANECDOTES.

166. Dies Præteritos.

Height, 3 8-10th inches; width, 2 3-10th inches.

167. Decoro inter verba Silentio.

Height, 3 8-10th inches; width, 2 3-10th inches.

168. Undé, undé, extricat.

Height, 3 8-10th inches; width, 2 3-10th inches.

169. COURTSHIP.

Height, 5 inches; width, 3 5-10th inches.

170. A LADY READING BY CANDLE-LIGHT.

Height, 4 1-10th inches; width, 2 6-10th inches.

Pub. by T. Cadell, 1787.

171. A SUBJECT UNKNOWN.

Height, 4 1-10th inches; width, 2 6-10th inches.

Pub. by T. Cadell, 1787.

172. AN INCANTATION SCENE.

Height, 4 1-10th inches; width, 2 6-10th inches.

Pub. by T. Cadell, 1787.

173. A LADY STANDING READING A LETTER.

Height, 4 1-10th inches; width, 2 6-10th inches.

Pub. by T. Cadell, 1787.

SPECTATOR.

174. **The Rosicrusian.** Vol. 5, No. 379. After Fuseli.

Height. 4 8-10th inches; width, 2 9-10th inches.

Pub. by John Sharpe, 1803.

175. **Theodosius and Constantia.** Vol. 2, No. 164. After Westall.

Height, 4 8-10th inches; width, 2 8-10th inches.

Pub. by John Sharpe, 1803.

LOWNDES' SHAKSPEARE.

176. **As you Like it.** Act 2, Scene 6.

Height, 5 inches; width, 3 5-10th inches.

177. **Macbeth.** Act 3, Scene 5.

Height, 5 inches; width, 3 5-10th inches.

178. **The Tempest.** Act 1, Scene 3.

Height, 5 inches; width, 3 5-10th inches.

179. **1st part, Henry IV.** Act 2, Scene 4.

Height, 5 inches; width, 3 5-10th inches.

180. **Cymbeline.** Act 3, Scene 1.

Height, 5 inches; width, 3 5-10th inches.

181. **Richard 3rd.** Act 5, Scene 3.

Height, 5 inches; width, 3 5-10th inches.

182. Merchant of Venice. Act 3, Scene 3.

Height, 5 inches; width, 3 5-10th inches.

BELL'S BRITISH THEATRE. Circles in ornamented rectangles.

Height, 5 inches; width, 3 3-10th inches.

183. Timon of Athens.

184. Julius Cæsar. Act 2, Scene 1.

185. The Provoked Husband. Act 5.

BELL'S BRITISH POETS. Circles in ornamented rectangles.

Height, 4 2-10th inches; width, 2 5-10th inches.

186. Alexander Pope, Esq'r.

187. Chaucer. Vol. VI.

188. Spencer. Vol. I.

189. Spencer. Book 5.

190. Cowley. Vol. II.

191. Tickle.

192. Waller. Vol. I.

193. Waller. Vol. II.

ICONOGRAPHY.

194. **Plate No. 97. Praise, Detraction, Contention, and Reconciliation.** Four designs. W. HAMILTON, DELT.

Height, 9 inches ; width, 7 inches.

195. **Plate No. 105. Temptation, Indulgence, Danger, and Security.** Four designs. W. HAMILTON, DELT.

Height, 9 inches ; width, 7 inches.

Pub. as the act directs, 17th April, 1779.

NOVELISTS, MAGAZINE, &c.

Height, 4 7-10th inches ; width, 2 8-10th inches.

196. **Alcibiades or the Self.** Vol. I.

197. **The Four Phials.** Vol. I.

198. **Soliman II.** Vol. I.

199. **By Good Luck.** Vol. I.

200. **All or Nothing.** Vol. I.

201. **The Scruple.** Vol. I.

202. **The Two Unfortunates.** Vol. I.

203. **Lausus & Lydia.** Vol. I.

204. **The School of Fathers.** Vol. II.

205. **The Shepherdess of the Alps.** Vol. II.

206. **Lauretta.** Vol. III.

207. **The Misanthrope corrected.** Vol. III.

208. **A Wife of Ten Thousand.** Vol. III.

209. **Chinese Tales.** STOTHARD, DEL.

210. **Tom Jones.** STOTHARD, DEL., 1780.

211. **Tom Jones.** STOTHARD, DEL., 1780.

212. **Gil Blas.** STOTHARD, DEL., 1781.

213. **Gil Blas.** STOTHARD, DEL., 1781.

214. **Subject unknown.**

CARD PLATES & TICKETS.

215. **W. Sharp, Engraver,** No. 9 Bartholomew Lane, Royal Exchange, London. Design, an angel seated among clouds.

216. **W. Sharp, Engraver.** History, ornamental writing, seals, &c. Design, two figures, one standing, the other seated on a cloud.

217. **Sharp, Carver & Guilder,** No. 44 Leadenhall street, London.

218. **Cockburn, Tobacconist & Snuff Maker,** No 146 Fenchurch Street.

219. **Jno. Wood.** The Post House, Ingatestone. Chaises & Horses.

220. **Will'm Robertson,** Trunk & Plate Case Maker, No. 14 New Bond Street.

221. **Lake, Engraver,** No. 9 Bartholomew Lane, Royal Exchange.

222. **Wm. Boreman, Watch & Clock Maker,** No. 8 Carthusian Street.

223. **Wm. Wilson, Bookseller and Stationer,** Dublin.

224. **Subscription Ticket,** for Ball at Carlisle House. Oblong oval.

Height, 4 inches; width, 5 2-10th inches.

225. **Subscription Ticket.** Carlisle House. Up. oval.

Height, 5 8-10th inches; width, 4 5-10th inches.

226. **Mr. Barthelemon's Night.** Design, Jeptha's Meeting with his Daughter. STOTHARD, DELT.

Height, 4 inches; width, 5 inches.

227. **Entrance Ticket,** for a Vauxhall Regatta.

228. **Orpheus and Eurydice.**

Height, 3 3-10th inches; width, 4 inches.

229. **Commerce.** Oblong oval encircled by a wreath.

Height, 4 7-10th inches; width, 8 inches.

230. **A Cherub,** seated among clouds.

Height, 2 7-10th inches; width, 3 1-10th inches.

231. **A Cherub,** flying.

Height, 3 inches; width, 2 8-10th inches.

TABLE

OF

SUBJECTS ALPHABETICALLY ARRANGED.

	No.
Agony of Christ, (The), ...	8
Alfred the Great dividing his loaf, &c. . . .	19
All or Nothing, ...	200
Alcibiades or the Self, ...	196
Angel destroying the Assyrian Camp, (The), .	1
Andrews, Joseph, ...	119
Annunciation to the Shepherds, ...	155
As you Like it. Act 2, Scene 6.	176
Assembly of the Heathen Deities on Mount Olympus, ...	159
Athens, ...	137
Barrington, Capt., ...	84
Barthelemon's Night, (Mr.), ...	226
Bentley, Richard, ...	93
Beresford, Mr., ...	63
Blas, Gil, ...	212

No.

Blas, Gil, ... 213

Blake, Robert, Admiral, ... 82

Boadicea haranguing the Britons, ... 17

Boadicea, the British Queen, animating the Britons, &c. 18

Boreman, Wm. Card, ... 222

Boulton, Matthew, ... 64

Bowyer's England, (Vignette for), ... 25

Britannia, ... 138

Brothers, Richard, ... 97

Brunton, Miss, as Monimia, ... 165

Burdett, Sir Francis, ... 40

Burney, Charles, D. D., ... 47

Bunyan, John, ... 94

Byng, George, Lord Torrington, ... 81

Cæsar, Julius. Act 2, Scene 1. 184

Carlisle House. Sub. Ticket for Ball, . . . 224

Carlisle House. Sub. Ticket, ... 225

Carter, Mr., ... 101

Cathcart, the Hon'ble Lt. Col. Charles, . . . 56

Chaucer. Vol. VI. 187

Chaucer, Reves Tale, ... 143

Charles the First. Portrait, ... 38

Charles the First. Interview with his children, &c., ... 20

No.

Charles the 2nd, landing on the beach at Dover, 21
Cherub, seated among clouds, ... 230
Cherub, flying, ... 231
Cherubim, from "The Doctors of the Church," 14
Children in the Wood, (The), ... 118
Chinese Tales, ... 209
Christ, head of. Ecce Homo, ... 9
Circe, ... 114
Clarence, Duke of, ... 72
Cleander bribing Cleon, ... 142
Cockburn, Tobacconist. Card, ... 218
Commerce. Card, ... 229
Contention, ... 194
Courtship, ... 169
Cowley. Vol. II., ... 190
Cromwell, Oliver, ... 75
Cymbeline. Act 3, Scene 1., ... 180
Cumberland, Richard, ... 92
Cuming, Guilelmus, M. D., ... 95
Cupid and his Mother, ... 111
Curtis, Sir William, ... 41
Danger, ... 195
Davis, Richard Hart, Esqr., ... 49
Decoro inter verba Silentio, ... 167
Detraction, ... 194

No.

Dies Præteritos, ... 166
Diogenes in Search of an Honest Man, . . . 27
Declaration of Rights, ... 123
Doctors of the Church, (The), ... 13
Dryden, ... 87
Dundas, The Right Hon'ble Robert, . . . 43
Eaton, Daniel Isaac, ... 96
Ecce Homo. Head of Christ, ... 9
Endor, The Witch of, ... 3
Erskine, The Hon'ble Thos., ... 86
Evil, ... 120
Family, The Holy, ... 6
Family, The Holy,—the smaller plate, . . . 7
Farquhar, Sir Walter, ... 42
Faulkner, Alderman Geo., ... 102
Forrest, Capt. Thos., ... 85
Foudroyant, The taking of the, ... 161
Garrick, David, ... 99
Gibraltar, Plan of, ... 162
Grecian Friezes, ... 151
Grecian Legend, Illustration of, ... 163
Greek Coins and Antiques, ... 150
Hamilton, Sir William, ... 77
Hapaéé, a Night Dance by Men in, ... 134
Hapaéé, a Night Dance by Women in, . . . 135

No.

Head of a Boy, from marble, ... 153
Head of a Female, from marble, ... 154
Head. Profile after Fuseli, ... 107
Head of an old Woman, after Rubens, . . . 108
Head of a Female, ... 109
Hector in the Tower, ... 115
Heidegger, C. The Musician. Mask, . . . 104
Heidegger. The Musician. Profile, ... 105
Henry IV., 1st Part. Act 2, Scene 4, . . . 179
Hero and Leander, ... 30
Home, Sir Everard, ... 52
Honywood, Filmer, Esq., ... 50
Howard, Thomas, Earl of Arundel, ... 39
Howe, Admiral Lord, ... 83
Hunter, John. Head, ... 53
Hunter, John, ... 54
Husband, The Provoked, ... 185
Hyde, The Hon'ble John, ... 44
Incantation Scene, ... 172
Indulgence, ... 195
Infant Christ, ... 4
Interview of Charles the First with his Children, &c., ... 20
Jenner, Edward, M. D., ... 51
Jerusalem Delivered. Tasso, ... 144

No.

Johnson, Dr. Samuel, ... 90
Johnson, John, ... 98
Jones, Tom, ... 210
Jones, Tom, ... 211
Judith Atireing, ... 2
Kamtschatka, a Man of, ... 125
Kamtschatka, a Woman of, ... 126
Kamtschatka, inside of a Winter Habitation in, 130
Kemble, ... 58
Kosciuszko, Thaddeus, ... 57
Lady Reading by Candle-light, ... 170
Lady Standing Reading a Letter, ... 173
Landscape with a Cottage, ... 116
Landscape, Hellesley Hill, ... 117
Lake, Engraver. Card, ... 221
Lauretta, ... 206
Lausus and Lydia, ... 203
Lear, King. Act 1, Scene 1, ... 31
Lear, King. Head after Reynolds, ... 32
Lear, King. Act III., Scene IV. "West," . 33
Long, Charles, ... 69
Louis VII., King of France, before Beckett's Tomb, ... 26
Luck, By Good, ... 199
Lucretia, ... 28

No.

Lunardi. The Balloonist, ... 106
Macbeth. Act 3, Scene 5. 177
Mangea, a Man of, ... 127
Maniacs, The Two, ... 121
Marys at the Sepulchre, (The), ... 10
Mary Magdalene, ... 12
Mary's, Q., Escape from Lochleven Castle, . . 22
Mask from the Antique, ... 152
Mayow Wynell—Mayow, Esqr., ... 66
Merchant of Venice. Act 3, Scene 3, . . . 182
Mercury putting on his Sandal Wings, . . . 148
Merry Wives of Windsor. Dr. Caius, . . . 35
Merry Wives of Windsor. Act V., Scene V., . 36
Milton, John, ... 88
Misanthrope Corrected, (The), ... 207
Monument to Hardinge, ... 122
Monk, George, Duke of Albemarle, ... 80
Moore, Samuel, ... 65
Moses Striking the Rock, ... 139
Nathan said unto David, ... 157
Nehemiah. Chap. II., V. III., ... 140
Newton, Sir Isaac, ... 91
Niobe, ... 113
Nootka Sound, a Man of, ... 128
Nootka Sound, a Woman of, ... 129

No.
Nootka Sound, The Inside of a House in, . . 131
Oonalashka, A Man of, ... 124
Oonalashka, The inside of a House in, . . . 132
Orpheus and Eurydice, ... 158
Orpheus and Eurydice. Card, ... 228
Pan and Syrinx, ... 141
Paine, Thomas, ... 61
Paine, Thomas. The smaller plate, ... 62
Persian Prince, ... 110
Phials, The Four, ... 197
Philosophy, The Muse of, ... 147
Poems, Frontispiece to. Ded. to her Majesty, . 160
Pope, Alexander, Esq'r, ... 186
Porson, Ricardus, ... 55
Portico of a Greek Temple, ... 149
Planta, Joseph, Esq'r, ... 103
Poulahol, King of the Friendly Islands, &c., . 133
Praise, ... 194
Raine, Matthew, D. D., ... 48
Raleigh, Sir Walter, ... 74
Reconciliation, ... 194
Reynolds, Richard, ... 67
Richard 3rd. Act 5, Scene 3, ... 37
Richard 3rd. Act 5, Scene 3. (Lowndes' Shakspeare, ... 181

No.
Robertson, Wm. Card, ... 220
Romeo and Juliet. Act III., Scene VII., . . . 34
Rosicrusian, The, ... 174
Savages, Two Nude, ... 136
Security, ... 195
School of Fathers, (The), ... 204
Scriptural Subject, ... 156
Seabury, The Right Reverend Samuel, D. D., . 46
Scruple, (The), ... 201
Shakspeare, Head of, ... 89
Sharp, William. Portrait, ... 59
Sharp, William. Card, ... 215
Sharp, W. Card, ... 216
Sharp, Guilder. Card, ... 217
Shepherdess of the Alps, (The), ... 205
Siddons, Mrs., as Euphrasia, ... 164
Soliman II., ... 198
Somerset, The Earl of, ... 145
Southcott, Joanna, ... 60
Spencer. Vol. I., ... 188
Spencer. Book 5, ... 189
St. Cecilia, ... 15
St. Cecilia. The small plate, ... 16
Sportsman, The Wounded, ... 146
Sortie made by the Garrison of Gibraltar, . . 23

No.

Siege and Relief of Gibraltar, ... 24
Temptation, ... 195
Tempest, (The). Act 1, Scene 3, ... 178
Tickle, ... 191
Timon of Athens, ... 183
Theodosius and Constantia, ... 175
Tooke, John Horne, ... 100
Undé, undé, extricat, ... 168
Unfortunates, The Two, ... 202
Unknown Subject, ... 171
Unknown Subject, ... 214
Vauxhall Regatta, Ticket for, ... 227
Venus and Europa, ... 112
Virgin and Infant Saviour, ... 5
Walker, Thomas, ... 68
Waller, Vol. I., ... 192
Waller, Vol. II., ... 193
Wales, George, Prince of, ... 70
Wales, George, Prince of. From a bust, . . . 71
Washington, George, Commander in Chief, &c., 73
Wharton, (Thomas, Marquis of), ... 78
Wife in ten thousand, (A), ... 208
Williamson, Robert Hopper, Esq'r, ... 45
Wilson, Wm. Card, ... 223
Women at the Sepulchre, (The), ... 11

No.

Wood, John. Card, ... 219

Wriothesley, Henry, Earl of Southampton, . . 76

Wynne, Sir John,. 79

Zenobia, ... 29

TABLE

OF

THE DATED PRINTS,

CHRONOLOGICALLY ARRANGED.

— 1775 —

Hector in the Tower. *Wm. Sharp, Pub.*

— 1777 —

Alderman George Faulkner.

— 1779 —

Capt. Thos. Forrest.
Iconography Plates.

— 1780 —

Circe. *John Boydell, Pub.*
George Washington.
Tom. Jones. Two Plates.

— *1781* —

Gil Blas. Two Plates.

— *1782* —

Alfred the Great dividing his loaf.
John Boydell, Pub.

Nehemiah. Chap. II., V. III.
Bell's British Library.

— *1783* —

Venus and Europa. *John Boydell, Pub.*

Romeo and Juliet. Act III., Scene VII.
John Boydell, Pub.

King Lear. Head. *John Boydell, Pub.*

Mrs. Siddons as Euphrasia. *W. Lowndes, Pub.*

The Two Maniacs.

— *1784* —

Lucretia. *John Boydell, Pub.*

Merry Wives of Windsor. Dr. Caius.
Chas. Taylor, Pub.

— *1785* —

The Doctors of the Church. *John Boydell, Pub.*

Gulielmus Cuming, M. D.

— 1786 —

The Children in the Wood. *Byrne & Medland, Pub.*

The Right Reverend Samuel Seabury, D. D. *T. S. Duche, Pub.*

Miss Brunton, as Monimia. *W. Lowndes, Pub.*

— 1787 —

Zenobia. *Wm. Sharp, Pub.*

Chaucer, Reves Tale.

An Incantation Scene. *T. Cadell, Pub.*

A Lady Reading by Candle-light. *T. Cadell, Pub.*

A Lady Standing Reading a Letter. *T. Cadell, Pub.*

— 1788 —

The Witch of Endor. *Thos. Macklin, Pub.*

Jos. Andrews. *W. Byrne, Pub.*

The Wounded Sportsman. *Pub. in a work of Miss Burney's.*

John Hunter. Head. *Wm. Sharp, Pub.*

John Hunter. ¾ length. *Wm. Sharp, Pub.*

— 1789 —

Cupid and his Mother.

King Charles the 2nd, Landing on the Beach at Dover. *B. West, &c., Pub.*

Oliver Cromwell. *T. Cadell, Pub.*

Henry Wriothesley, Earl of Southampton. *J. Rivington, Pub.*

— 1790 —

St. Cecilia. *Wm. Sharp, Pub.*

George, Prince of Wales. *Wm. Sharp, Pub.*

The Right Hon'ble Robert Dundas. *Wm. Sharp, Pub.*

— 1791 —

The Agony of Christ. "*Macklin's Bible.*"

The Marys at the Sepulchre. "*Macklin's Bible.*"

The Hon'ble Lt. Col. Charles Cathcart.

The Hon'ble Thos. Erskine. *Wm. Sharp, Pub.*

George, Prince of Wales. From a bust.

— 1792 —

The Angel Destroying the Assyrian Camp. "*Macklin's Bible.*"

The Holy Family. *Thos. Macklin, Pub.*

Niobe. *S. Smith, Pub.*

Diogenes in Search of an Honest Man. *Wm. Sharp, Pub.*

King Lear. Act III., Scene IV. B. West. *J. & J. Boydell, Pub.*

King Lear. Act I., Scene I. R. Smirke. *J. & J. Boydell, Pub.*

— *1793* —

The Holy Family. The smaller plate.
"Macklin's Bible."

Merry Wives of Windsor. Act V., Scene V.
J. & J. Boydell, Pub.

Thomas Paine.

— *1794* —

Judith Atireing. *"Macklin's Bible."*

Richard 3rd. Act 5, Scene 3.
Mr. Woodmason, Pub.

Daniel Isaac Eaton.

Thomas Paine. The Smaller plate.
Wm. Sharp, Pub.

Thomas Walker. *Wm. Sharp, Pub.*

— *1795* —

Boadicea, haranguing the Britons.
"Bowyer's, England."

Q. Mary's Escape from Lochleven Castle.
"Bowyer's, England."

Richard Brothers, "Prince of the Hebrews."
Wm. Sharp, Pub.

— *1796* —

Mr. Beresford. *Wm. Sharp, Pub.*

— *1797* —

The Virgin and Infant Saviour. *Wm Sharp, Pub.*

Head of Christ, crowned with Thorns.
Wm Sharp, Pub.

— *1798* —

Mercury putting on his sandal wings. Frontispiece to "Diversions of Purley."
John Horne Tooke, Pub.

— *1799* —

The Sortie made by the Garrison of Gibraltar, in the morning of the 27th of November, 1781.
J. Trumbull, W. Sharp, &c., Pub.

— *1800* —

Louis VII., King of France, before Beckett's Tomb.
"*Bowyer's, England.*"

Vignette for Bowyer's England.

The Hon'ble John Hyde.
R. Home & W. Sharp, Pub.

Thaddeus Kosciuszko. *C. Andras, Pub.*

— *1801* —

Matthew Boulton, Esqr. *Wm. Sharp, Pub.*

— *1802* —

An Assembly of the Heathen Deities on Mt. Olympus. *Verner & Hood, Pub.*

— *1803* —

Kemble. *Wm. Sharp, Pub.*

The Rosicrusian. Spectator. *John Sharpe, Pub.*

Theodosius and Constantia. Spectator. *John Sharpe, Pub.*

— *1804* —

Filmer Honywood, Esq'r, M. P. *Wm. Sharp, Pub.*

— *1810* —

The Siege and Relief of Gibraltar. *J. S. Copley, Pub.*

Admiral Lord Howe. *J. S. Copley, Pub.*

Capt. Barrington. *J. S. Copley, Pub.*

Sir Everard Home. *Wm. Sharp, Pub.*

Ricardus Porson. *Wm. Sharp, Pub.*

— *1811* —

Boadicea, the British Queen, animating the Britons to defend their country against the Romans. *Wm. Sharp, Pub.*

Sir Francis Burdett, Bart. *Wm. Sharp, Pub.*

— *1812* —

Joanna Southcott. *Jane Townley, Pub.*

— *1813* —

Charles the First, King of Great Britain, &c.
W. Buchanan, Pub.

Monument to Hardinge. *Sarah Manning, Pub.*

— *1814* —

St. Cecilia. The small plate. *Ar. Stone, Pub.*

Thomas Howard, Earl of Arundel.
W. Buchanan, Pub.

Sir William Curtis, Bart. *W. S. Blake, Pub.*

— *1815* —

Matthew Raine, D. D. *Wm. Sharp, Pub.*

— *1816* —

Evil. *Wm. Sharp, Pub.*

— *1817* —

William Sharp. *John Smith, Pub.*

Richard Reynolds. *W. Hobday, Pub.*

Joseph Planta, Esqr. *W. Clark, Pub.*

— *1818* —

The Interview of Charles the First with his children, &c. *W. Sharp, Pub.*

— *1819* —

John Bunyan. *Hurst, Robinson & Co., Pub.*

— *1820* —

Mary Magdalene. *W. Sharp, Pub.*

— *1821* —

Infant Christ. *W. Miller, Pub.*

Charles Burney, D. D.

— *1822* —

The Women at the Sepulchre. Left unfinished. *W. Sharp, Pub.*

— *1823* —

David Garrick. *W. Walker, Pub.*

www.ingramcontent.com/pod-product-compliance
Lightning Source LLC
LaVergne TN
LVHW021426110826
845150LV00007B/2104

* 9 7 8 1 4 2 5 5 0 8 8 8 3 *